To Jim, Geneva, and Jennifer Donald

Thank you for your love for First Baptist Church Dallas
and your vision for Pathway to Victory
as we work together "to transform the world
with the truth of God's Word."

You are an incomparable encouragement
to your pastor.

COURAGEOUS

10 STRATEGIES for THRIVING
in a HOSTILE WORLD

DR. ROBERT
JEFFRESS

BakerBooks
a division of Baker Publishing Group
Grand Rapids, Michigan

Published by Baker Books
a division of Baker Publishing Group
PO Box 6287, Grand Rapids, MI 49516-6287
www.bakerbooks.com

Printed in the United States of America

Library of Congress Cataloging-in-Publication Data
Names: Jeffress, Robert, 1955– author.
Title: Courageous : 10 strategies for thriving in a hostile world / Dr. Robert Jeffress.
Description: Grand Rapids : Baker Books, a division of Baker Publishing Group, 2020. |
Identifiers: LCCN 2019028739 | ISBN 9780801075391 (cloth)
Subjects: LCSH: Courage—Religious aspects—Christianity. | Christianity and culture.
Classification: LCC BV4647.C75 J44 2020 | DDC 241/.4—dc23
LC record available at https://lccn.loc.gov/2019028739

Published in association with Yates & Yates, www.yates2.com.

20 21 22 23 24 25 26   7 6 5 4 3 2 1

Jeffress shows us page-by-page how to live as winsome and effective ambassadors for Jesus Christ, all so that the perishing will come to salvation and God will receive the glory! I give this book a double thumbs-up!"

Joni Eareckson Tada, Joni and Friends
International Disability Center

"No book title ever fit its author's personality better than this one. One of the words I often use to describe Robert Jeffress is *courageous*. As a former pastor of First Baptist in Dallas, I have been privileged to watch time and again his courageous yet loving leadership in daily action. This book is not some self-help treatise. These principles have been beaten out on the anvil of the author's own personal and practical experience. Read it . . . and reap!"

O. S. Hawkins, author of the bestselling Code series
of Christian devotionals

"My friend Robert Jeffress has demonstrated courage time and again by boldly preaching God's Word in the pulpit and answering tough critics in the media. In these pages, he outlines practical survival strategies that will help us courageously navigate the storms of life. Through powerful biblical examples and present-day testimonies, Robert reminds us that the wisdom and supernatural ability God has provided us as believers is more than enough to defeat the enemy's strategy."

James Robison, founder and president of LIFE Outreach
International, Fort Worth, Texas

"If you are a follower of Jesus Christ, this is a must-read book! Though I have taught survival skills to Marines, Boy Scouts, my four kids, and now eighteen grandkids, it never occurred to me to apply these skills to living as a Christian in today's hostile environment. Thankfully, my friend Dr. Jeffress did—just in time."

Lt. Col. Oliver North, USMC (Ret.)

"It's one thing to say we have faith and another thing entirely to know how to live out that faith! In *Courageous*, my friend Robert Jeffress beautifully helps us understand how to put our faith into real action in our lives—which is of course the whole point!"

Eric Metaxas, author of the #1 *New York Times* bestseller *Bonhoeffer: Pastor, Martyr, Prophet, Spy* and host of the *Eric Metaxas Show*

"With all the uncertainty in our world right now, this new book by my friend Robert Jeffress is a welcome encouragement for believers. His Bible-based tips on thriving during challenging times are not only practical and easy to understand but will help you to stand strong in your faith and live victoriously."

Robert Morris, founding lead senior pastor of Gateway Church and bestselling author of *The Blessed Life*, *Frequency*, and *Beyond Blessed*

"When it comes to living out biblical principles, we quickly discover we're in an unfriendly culture. Ephesians 5:11 tells us to 'Have nothing to do with the fruitless deeds of darkness,' so how then do we build bridges to skeptics and cynics? How do we win wicked people with antagonistic agendas to the side of our Savior? In his remarkable new book, *Courageous: 10 Strategies for Thriving in a Hostile World*, Dr.

Contents

Acknowledgments

Occasionally people will ask me how I manage to be involved in so many different avenues of ministry. The simple answer is that it would be impossible if it were not for the tremendously gifted and dedicated team I've been blessed to work with. That team includes . . .

Brian Vos, Mark Rice, Brianna DeWitt, Lindsey Spoolstra, and the entire Baker Books team, who are the best publishing partner I've ever worked with.

Derrick G. Jeter, our creative director at Pathway to Victory, and Jennifer Stair, who were instrumental in crafting the message of this book.

Sealy Yates, my literary agent and friend for more than two decades, who always provides encouragement and wise counsel.

Carrilyn Baker, my extraordinary executive associate for nearly two decades, who provides limitless efforts in overseeing all of the complicated work of our office—and always does so with a wonderful attitude. And thank you, Mary

Shafer, for assisting Carrilyn and me in innumerable ways— you are a joy to work with!

Ben Lovvorn, the executive pastor of First Baptist Church, Dallas, and Nate Curtis, Patrick Heatherington, Ben Bugg, and the entire Pathway to Victory team, who extend the message of this book to millions of people throughout the world.

I'm eternally grateful for the support I receive every day from my family. God has blessed me with two wonderful daughters, Julia and Dorothy, a great son-in-law, Ryan Sadler, and my extraordinary triplet grandchildren, Barrett, Blake, and Blair.

But at the very top of the list of those people in my life for whom I am most grateful is my wife of forty-two years, Amy. Thank you for your unconditional love. You are the greatest evidence to me of God's goodness and grace.

Introduction

A Survival Guide for Christians

As a pastor, author, and news contributor, I travel a lot. My travels have taken me around the world—including the former Soviet Union, Europe, the Middle East, and all over North America. During the millions of air miles I've logged, I've encountered my share of turbulence and bad weather, and I've sat in aircraft that looked less sturdy than the rubber band–powered balsa wood planes I used to build as a kid. But never once, in all my years of flying, have I truly worried that I might not survive a flight and make it back in one piece.

After untold hours of listening to flight attendants give safety instructions, I've never needed to put on my oxygen mask before helping other passengers with theirs. I have not opened an emergency exit door or used my seat cushion as a flotation device. And though I think it would be quite a memorable experience, I have never slid down an inflatable rescue ramp.

Thankfully, during all my travels around the world, I haven't experienced any situation in which I had to make a decision that could mean the difference between life and death. But that's not the case with the people you will read about in this book. Each chapter opens with a true story that illustrates one of ten survival tips that are critical to make it out of life-threatening situations alive. These essential tips are:

1. Don't panic.
2. Gain situational awareness.
3. Take inventory.
4. Develop a victor, not a victim mindset.
5. Trust your training.
6. Bend, don't break.
7. Beware of celebrating the summit.
8. Learn from the past.
9. Help others.
10. Do the next right thing.

Now, I'm not a survivalist; I'm a pastor. So obviously this book isn't intended to be a manual for surviving a plane crash or trekking across a desert with an empty canteen. You won't find tips on how to start a fire with a battery and a gum wrapper, how to navigate by the stars, or how to purify water to make it safe to drink.

But most of the struggles you and I face in life have nothing to do with plane crashes, shipwrecks, or burning buildings.

Instead, as Christians, we must learn how to survive the daily challenges of living out our faith in this complicated world. It's easy to get stuck in survival mode, just trying to figure out how to make it through each day. But the life that God calls us to is so much more! In this book, you will find practical tips on how to have courageous faith in a culture that is opposed to God and His truth, as well as the biblical answers, encouragement, and hope you need to thrive in your own personal struggles.

You see, what is true in survival situations—a soldier behind enemy lines, a mountain climber caught in a blizzard, or a sailor on dangerous seas—is equally true of followers of Jesus living in an increasingly secular world. Like all survivors, we must not allow ourselves to become sidelined by fear. Instead, we can choose to rely on certain learned skills to make it through stressful circumstances and difficult environments.

The pages that follow are filled with stories of men and women whose courage and coolheaded responses helped them survive seemingly hopeless situations. As you read their stories, you will discover that survivors not only have a different response to troubles but also have a different perspective on life.

Jesus never taught that Christianity is an automatic exemption from trials. In fact, difficulties are part of the price we pay for living in this world. Consider Christ's words in John 16:33: "These things I have spoken to you, so that in Me you may have peace. In the world you have tribulation, but *take courage*; I have overcome the world." Notice that Jesus didn't say that we would live without problems; instead, He offers us a way to thrive despite our problems.

In *Courageous*, we will look at ten survival strategies that Christians must use to navigate the tumultuous terrain of today's world. My prayer is that this book will strengthen your courage by serving as a kind of spiritual compass to guide you, with true north pointing to Christ.

Don't Panic

The flight from Columbus, Ohio, to Los Angeles, California, was routine. Aboard USAirways 1493, David Koch sat shoeless in first-class compartment seat 2A. As the airliner neared Los Angeles International Airport, he looked out the window as the sun began to set over the Pacific Ocean. They would be landing soon.

I probably ought to put on my shoes, he thought, but he decided to wait. On their final approach, David watched the sun sink below the horizon. Moments later, he felt the familiar jolt and heard the screech of the tires as the 737 jumbo jet, carrying eighty-three passengers and six crewmembers, touched down on LAX's Runway 24 Left.

Then David heard "a sudden, sickening crunch." Sparks hurtled past his window, followed by the bright flash of a fireball. Screams filled the aircraft as a flight attendant shouted, "Stay down!"

As the plane skidded along the runway, David unbuckled his seat belt to prepare for a quick exit. The plane came to a violent stop, and another explosion rocked the cabin, throwing him forward into the first row of seats and then into the bulkhead. The fuselage went dark and began filling with smoke. No instructions came from the pilot or flight attendants. Passengers were on their own, running toward the back of the plane.

"I immediately got on my hands and knees and attempted to find my shoes," David recalled. "I believed it would be difficult to escape a burning plane in my stocking feet." But his shoes were nowhere to be found.

Trying to stay under the smoke, David crawled toward the back of the plane. In a panic, other passengers trampled him. "I encountered a fighting, frenzied mob jamming the aisle," he later said. "Escape was probably impossible because I was last in line to get out the rear exit. I concluded that I was probably going to die. At that point I stood up and, choking heavily on smoke, walked back toward the first-class section."

"I was not panicked nor was I terrified," David remembered. He was resigned. "For a few long moments I stood there, immobilized, not knowing what else to do, and I knew with absolute certainty that I was going to die." Then it came to him: if smoke was coming in from the front of the plane, then there had to be an opening that might offer a way of escape.

David worked his way toward the cockpit, but seeing flames lick the passenger door, he realized that was an impossible route. On the verge of passing out—he guessed he had maybe ten or fifteen seconds before he fell unconscious—he turned to the opposite wall and saw a crack in the fuselage. He wedged his fingers into it and pulled. It was the galley door, and it opened to the outside. He thrust his head through and gulped a few breaths of air. "A tremendous sense of strength came over me, and a wave of adrenaline shot through my body," he said.

David looked down and saw a fire burning under the airplane. To clear the flames, he jumped away from the wreckage and hit the asphalt ten feet below. Other survivors were scattered about. Some sobbed, some were silent, and some stared in disbelief at the burning aircraft.

"I consider it a miracle that I escaped," David said, "and that I came through the ordeal as well as I did."[1]

Do Not Panic   *fight or fright*

The number-one rule in any survival situation is this: don't panic. Studies have shown that when most people—those of us without military, first responder, or survivalist training—are faced with a threatening situation, about 10 percent of men and women have a *fight* response. They are able to gain control of their emotions and determine the right course of action to survive. Another 10 percent have a *flight* response. They lose control of their emotions and panic, which causes them to do things that are harmful to themselves and others. The remaining 80 percent *freeze*. They become emotionally overwhelmed, unable to do anything at all.[2]

David demonstrated the fight response in his escape from USAirways Flight 1493. But other people apparently had flight and freeze responses. Investigators who interviewed survivors were told that the passenger in 10F—an emergency row—froze in fear and was unable to open the exit door. The passenger in 11D climbed over the seats, unfastened the latch, and pushed her through the opening onto the wing, saving her life. A few moments later, two passengers began fighting about who would exit next. The altercation lasted only a few seconds, but it slowed the evacuation. In both instances, panic led to unnecessary deaths.

As I read the story of USAirways Flight 1493, I found myself wondering, *What would I have done if I were a passenger on that plane?* What would *you* have done? Thankfully, you and I will probably not have to make a life-or-death decision while trying to escape a burning aircraft. But that doesn't mean we won't face other fearful situations.

Think for a moment about what you fear most in life. What are some of your greatest worries? I imagine that many of your fears involve something being taken away from you—a person, a position, or a possession. Maybe you are afraid that you will lose a loved one through death or desertion. Perhaps you are worried about losing your job and, as a result, your prestige and financial stability. Or maybe you are fearful about losing your health or physical well-being.

Parents fear their children will become enslaved to addictions such as drugs, alcohol, or pornography. Young adults fear they will not be able to find well-paying jobs that allow them to live independently from their parents (some parents share that same fear!). Middle-aged men and women, who have more years behind them than ahead, fear their lives won't count for much. Senior citizens are afraid of being lonely. And Christians of all ages look at current events and worry that our culture is unraveling. You could add your own personal and particular fears to that list.

The truth is, there are seemingly endless situations that tempt us to fear in this life. Whether it is the corroding effects of our culture or the issues that confront our hearts and homes, this world can be a frightening and dangerous place. However, if we are to survive when challenges come, *we must not panic.*

Keep Calm and Carry On

Sometimes, when I have an evening at home, I enjoy snacking on a bowl of popcorn while watching the news or a television program. Not long ago, I tuned in to a fascinating historical documentary about an event that illustrates this survival principle.

At the start of World War II, when Britain stood virtually alone against Nazi Germany, the Ministry of Information printed a series of three posters designed to prevent people from panicking. The first poster read, "Freedom Is in Peril; Defend It with All Your Might." The second said, "Your Courage, Your Cheerfulness, Your Resolution Will Bring Us Victory." Thousands of these two posters were plastered all over Britain.

A third poster was printed but not distributed, intended to be used only if Germany invaded Britain. In bold, white letters printed against a red background, and proudly displaying the royal crown, the third poster simply read: "Keep Calm and Carry On."[3] Of course, that is easier said than done, especially when bombs are falling on your head! But this message is more than British stiff-upper-lip propaganda. It can help us maintain a proper perspective on fear, no matter what circumstances we may be facing.

We can see the idea of "Keep Calm and Carry On" throughout the New Testament, especially in the book of 1 Peter. The apostle Peter wrote this letter to Christians who were being slandered and shunned because they dared to live faithfully for Christ in a pagan society. In the face of increasing persecution, Peter encouraged believers to remember two things: first, the world is hostile to Christians, and second, the grace of God is sufficient to deal with these hostilities.

How to Live in an Anti-Christian World

The culture in which the first-century believers lived was dominated by values and beliefs that were contrary to Christianity. According to Peter, many people were indulging in "sensuality, lusts, drunkenness, carousing, drinking parties and abominable idolatries" (1 Pet. 4:3). They were "surprised" that followers of Jesus "[did] not run with them into the same excesses of dissipation" (v. 4). As a result, they ridiculed and maligned Christians who didn't participate in their immorality.

Not much has changed in two thousand years, has it?

When Peter wrote this letter to encourage the early believers to stand firm in the grace of God, he gave two commands that are just as relevant to us today.

Be Disciplined in Your Thinking

First, Peter said that for Christians to live holy lives, we need to be disciplined in our thinking. In 1 Peter 1:13, he wrote, "Prepare your minds for action."

The mind is extremely important—it functions as command central for the rest of the body. That's why the Bible continually talks about the importance of right thinking. For example, Romans 12:2 says, "Do not be conformed to this world, but be transformed *by the renewing of your mind,* so that you may prove what the will of God is, that which is good and acceptable and perfect." And Philippians 4:8 admonishes us, "Whatever is true, whatever is noble, whatever is right, whatever is pure, whatever is lovely, whatever is admirable—if anything is excellent or praiseworthy—*think* about such things" (NIV).

A church member once told me that every night he used to watch cable news before he went to bed. He said it made him so anxious and depressed that he decided to stop watching the news before he went to sleep. You know what he does now? He listens to sermons before he goes to bed. He said, "Pastor, it's the most amazing thing. I drift off to sleep listening to those messages, and then I sleep well all night." (He's not the only one who has fallen asleep listening to my messages!) Seriously, though, this person has learned one practical benefit of filling our minds with the Word of God.

If we are going to "prepare [our] minds for action" (1 Pet. 1:13), then we need to refuse to fill our minds with things that tempt us to fear. And that means controlling the sights, sounds, and experiences that go into our brains. What kinds of input are you storing in your mind? The things you allow into your mind eventually will affect your actions. As believers, we must make every effort to keep our minds free from things that could cause us to compromise our commitment to Christ.

Let's be honest: today's culture is filled with distractions that, if we are not careful, can lead us away from the things of God. I remember a time when I got distracted, and it led me into trouble. When I was five years old, my father took me to the State Fair of Texas—the largest fair of its kind in the country. As we were about to enter the midway, my dad stopped at the restroom and said, "Robert, wait out here for me. I'll be right back." I stood there for what seemed to be an eternity, waiting for my dad. But the bells and whistles of the midway were too much for me to resist, and I wandered away. Soon, I was completely lost. I still remember the terror of that moment, being surrounded by strangers in an unfamiliar place. Fortunately, a police officer noticed me and placed me on the back of his three-wheeled motorcycle to take me to the lost and found. And fortunately, as we weaved through the midway crowd, my dad spotted me on the back of the motorcycle and started running toward me. When he reached the motorcycle he literally swept me off the back of the vehicle into his arms. Why did I wander away from my dad? I was distracted by the midway instead of being disciplined in my thinking and obedient to my father.

In the hymn "Come, Thou Fount of Every Blessing," one of the refrains says, "Prone to wander, Lord, I feel it."[4] It's true: you and I are prone to be distracted by any number of things in this world, and we end up wandering away from our heavenly Father. That's why Peter said that if you and I are going to survive in this world with our faith intact, we must be disciplined in keeping our thoughts centered on God and His truth.

Be Disciplined in Your Conduct

Second, if we are going to survive as followers of Christ in this world, Peter said we need to be disciplined in our conduct. In 1 Peter 1:13, he wrote, "Keep sober in spirit."

In other words, we are to be calm, steady, and controlled—not giving in to our "former lusts" (v. 14). Instead, we are to pursue a life that is pleasing to God.

Peter continued, "Like the Holy One who called you, be holy yourselves also in all your behavior; because it is written, 'You shall be holy, for I am holy'" (vv. 15–16). The word *holy* means "separate." If you are a Christian, that means you are to live separately and in a different way from the unbelievers around you.

Now, I don't have to tell you that living a holy life in this world is no easy task. That's why Romans 13:14 tells us, "Make no provision for the flesh in regard to its lusts." If you are going to resist temptation, you cannot make an allowance for sin. You are going to have to run as far and as fast from temptation as you can. Your choices may look different from those of your friends, your coworkers, or your neighbors—but if you are committed to living a life that pleases God, you will choose to honor Him in your thoughts, words, and actions.

"Wait a minute, Pastor," you may be saying. "Do you mean that to survive as a Christian in this world, I have to separate myself from sinful people?" Of course not! Where on earth could you go where there would be no sinners? It is not only impossible to separate yourself from unbelievers but it is also unbiblical to do so. In John 17:15, Jesus prayed for us, "I do not ask You to take them out of the world, but to keep them from the evil one."

God has called us to be "ambassadors for Christ" (2 Cor. 5:20). We cannot be an ambassador to people if we are not spending time with them! As Jesus's representatives in this world, we are called not only to communicate God's message of salvation but also to influence our culture with God's truth.

So how can we live holy lives in the midst of today's secular world? It's a matter of perspective. Are you primarily concerned with the things of earth, or are you keeping your focus on Jesus Christ? In 1 Peter 1:13, Peter said that believers can stand firm in our conduct when we "fix [our] hope *completely* on the grace to be brought to [us] at the revelation of Jesus Christ." Our anticipation of Christ's return strengthens our faith and gives us hope during difficult days.

I know what it feels like to anticipate the return of someone I love. Though it was decades ago, I distinctly remember being in a chapel service during my freshman orientation at Baylor University in Waco, Texas. My girlfriend (now my wife) was one hundred miles away at the University of Texas in Austin. It was the first time we had been separated in our four years of dating, and I was miserable. We would not be able to see one another for two whole weeks. I was counting the minutes until Amy and I were reunited!

In much the same way, the Bible says, we are to eagerly anticipate the return of the One who loves us the most: the Lord Jesus Christ. But until that glorious day comes, Peter said, we remain on this earth "as aliens and strangers" (1 Pet. 2:11).

Enemy-Occupied Territory

As our nation moves further and further away from its Christian foundation, believers in America are increasingly experiencing the sense that we are aliens in a foreign country. Living in a culture that mocks biblical values and accepts immorality can make us feel as if we are surrounded by strangers speaking an unfamiliar language. We are living, as C. S. Lewis put it, in "enemy-occupied territory—that is what this world is."[5]

Being an outsider in a hostile land can be frightening. Many years ago, when I was a youth minister, I took a group of teenagers to the Soviet Union for a mission trip. It was during the Cold War, and the atmosphere was so oppressive that we couldn't wait to get out of there. On the day we were to leave Russia, I got caught on the wrong side of the customs line without my passport. I explained my predicament to the Soviet agent, but he was very clear: no passport, no exit. Those few minutes before my passport turned up were some of the scariest moments in my life. I still shiver when I think about what might have happened if I hadn't found my passport.

As Christians, we are to conduct ourselves not as citizens of the culture in which we live but as citizens of the culture we represent—heaven.

Stand Firm in Grace

The world system has always been hostile to the Christian faith. It was true two thousand years ago, when Peter penned his letter to the believers in Asia Minor, and it is true today, as I pen this book to believers in the United States and across the globe. The world is not our friend. But that is no reason for us to panic! We do not have to fear the world, because God's grace is sufficient to overcome the world's opposition to Him and His truth.

Peter concluded his letter with these words: "This is the true grace of God. Stand firm in it!" (1 Pet. 5:12). Grace is the overriding theme of 1 Peter. The word *grace* occurs in every chapter, because grace is the thing we need most when we go through difficult circumstances.

Since grace is essential to our lives as believers, it's important that we understand exactly what grace is. What do we mean when we talk about grace? When we are speaking of our salvation, grace is God's undeserved favor. Though there are many ways to explain it, I particularly like this definition: "Grace is God's burst of undeserved generosity."[6] Grace is God giving us what we don't deserve: eternal life.

But grace is more than that. It also refers to God's supernatural help. For those of us who have received God's gift of salvation, when we go through suffering or trials, God gives us His grace—His divine assistance—to supply us with the strength we need. Peter had this kind of grace in mind when he urged believers to stand firm in grace.

The apostle Paul described a time when he experienced God's supernatural help. He said that he was given "a thorn in the flesh, a messenger of Satan to torment me" (2 Cor. 12:7). Satan's message to Paul was pain and panic. But the Lord's message to him was grace: "My grace is sufficient for you, for power is perfected in weakness" (v. 9). Three times, Paul asked God to take away this "thorn." Instead, God gave Paul what he needed most—His help. As a result, Paul did not simply endure his suffering; he rose above his suffering. By God's grace, Paul was able to write, "Most gladly, therefore, I will rather boast about my weaknesses, so that the power of Christ may dwell in me" (v. 9).

This was the message Peter wrote to the first-century believers. And it is the same message you and I need to hear today. God's grace is more than enough to help us rise above the fears that tend to grip our hearts. The promise of God's grace stiffens our spiritual spines with courage. This is great news, because make no mistake about it, storms will come—either literally, as when brave men and women across our nation face devastating hurricanes and floods, or figuratively, as when our culture outlaws any mention of God in the public square or when your spouse files for divorce.

No matter what storms we face, they almost always bring a rising tide of panic. And when the wind is howling, either outside our windows or inside our hearts, you and I need to hear a message of courage, like the one Paul delivered to his frightened shipmates after their vessel crashed: "'Do not be afraid.' . . . Keep up your courage" (Acts 27:24–25).

Without courage, the difficulties of this life would cause us to despair. This is why we must never let fear gain a foothold. "Fear and faith can't live together very long in the same heart," observed Bible teacher Warren Wiersbe. "Either fear will conquer faith and we'll quit, or faith will conquer fear and we'll triumph."[7]

Joshua: An Example of Courage

The Bible is filled with stories of ordinary people who overcame fear with faith. One of my favorite examples is Joshua, Moses's protégé. Standing at the Jordan River and peering into the promised land, Joshua trembled at the task he had been given. Moses had died, leaving Joshua as the new leader of Israel. But how was Joshua supposed to fill the sandals of Moses—the man who spoke face-to-face with God and led Israel for forty years?

I know a little of what Joshua must have felt. In 2018, the church I pastor, First Baptist Church of Dallas, celebrated its 150th anniversary. This church was established by great men and women of God. Over the years, many gifted preachers have filled its pulpit. Perhaps the greatest of these was my mentor and pastor Dr. W. A. Criswell, who delivered God's inerrant Word to First Baptist Dallas for fifty years. When I stood in the historic sanctuary of First Baptist Dallas to deliver my first sermon as senior pastor, standing in the same spot as the legendary pastor had stood, I felt insignificant and afraid. How was I going to fill Dr. Criswell's shoes?

In time, I learned that God's kingdom work always goes on. For me, that meant stepping into the pulpit and continuing Dr. Criswell's legacy of faithfully preaching God's Word. For Joshua, that meant leading the Israelites into the promised land and defeating the enemies there. For you, it will mean something else. You may not be thrust into a position of responsibility, following on the heels of a beloved leader. But God will lead you into places where you encounter people and tasks that are larger than you. Whenever this happens, whether in your job, your family, or your spiritual life, it can be terrifying. You will be tempted to panic and run in the opposite direction or be frozen by fear. Instead, God wants you to summon the courage to obey Him by taking that first step into the unknown.

God's command to Joshua could have easily sent him into a full-blown panic attack—it certainly would have unnerved most of us, had we been in his place! The Lord said to Joshua,

"Moses My servant is dead; now therefore arise, cross this Jordan, you and all this people, to the land which I am giving to them, to the sons of Israel" (Josh. 1:2). This command was filled with danger. Joshua would have to march down the steep eastern bank of the Jordan Valley, cross the river at flood stage, ascend the western bank, and attack an army of "men of great size" (Num. 13:32). No wonder he was shaking in his sandals!

Three Reasons to Take Courage

A frightened leader can do more harm to a group of people than an enemy horde. Leadership experts sometimes refer to this as the "headless chicken" syndrome, when a leader's observable fear during a crisis causes people to run around in a panic, and nobody knows what they are supposed to do.

While fear is an understandable response to danger, the good news is that all of us can learn how to take courage during difficult times. Leadership blogger Seth Godin explained, "Fear is a natural reaction to risk. While risk is real and external, fear exists only in our imagination. Fear is the workout we give ourselves imagining what will happen if things don't work out." He went on to say, "It's possible to have risk (a good thing) without debilitating fear or its best friend, obsessive worry."[8]

So to embolden His timid leader and keep panic from spreading throughout the camp, God gave Joshua three limitless resources that would provide the new leader with courage: God's promises, God's Word, and God's presence.

Courage from God's Promises

God commanded Joshua to lead the people into the promised land, to defeat the enemies there, and to divide the land according to tribe. This was a huge undertaking, especially for a new leader. But God doesn't give us commands without also providing the resources we need to obey those commands. So God gave Joshua three promises, one for each task.

First, *God promised that the Israelites would enter the land.* He said to Joshua, "Every place on which the sole of your foot treads, I have given it to you, just as I spoke to Moses. From the wilderness and this Lebanon, even as far as the great river, the river Euphrates, all the land of the Hittites, and as far as the Great Sea [the Mediterranean] toward the setting of the sun will be your territory" (Josh. 1:3–4). God promised to lead the way across the Jordan River and give His people everything they needed to claim the land. If the Lord has called you to a new task and you step out in faith, then you can rest assured that what He has promised, He will fulfill.

I remember when God called me to a new task that required me to step out in faith—my first invitation to contribute to a national news program. At the time, I was pastoring a church in the small city of Wichita Falls, Texas. *Who am I to appear on this show and speak God's truth to a national audience?* I wondered. Although I sensed that God was calling me to accept the invitation, I have to admit that I balked when I considered the criticism I would surely receive from the mainstream media. Then I remembered that somebody once said there are three guaranteed ways to avoid criticism:

do nothing, say nothing, and be nothing. All true leaders are going to face criticism. I realized that the question I had to answer wasn't, Will I be criticized for doing this? It was, Am I willing to obey God no matter what others might say?

After much prayer, I concluded that what God had called me to do, He would equip me to fulfill. I decided to go on the news program and speak God's truth. Since that time, God has given me thousands of opportunities to proclaim His truth on major media outlets to millions of viewers, some of whom would never attend a church. But it all started many years ago, when I sensed God's call to a new task and, despite my inexperience and concerns, decided to respond with faith instead of fear.

What new task has God called you to do? What have you sensed the Holy Spirit leading you to do, but you think, *I could never do that*? You can respond to that seemingly impossible task with either faith or fear. Perhaps right now you can only see the difficulty of your circumstances. But alongside that reality is another reality: God Himself will be with you, surrounding and protecting you as you follow Him.

Second, *God promised that Israel would be victorious over their enemies.* God told Joshua, "No one will be able to stand against you all the days of your life. As I was with Moses, so I will be with you; I will never leave you nor forsake you" (Josh. 1:5 NIV). Hearing these words must have given Joshua courage.

Every Christian has enemies to fight. It's easy for us to think of those enemies as being "out there"—in the culture. But in reality, our fiercest battles are with the enemies "in here"—with the sin nature that, though defeated, still resides in our own hearts. We wrestle with fear, worry, depression, doubt, anxiety, and a number of other struggles that seem to persist no matter how hard we pray. And the struggle is never-ending. Yet God has promised to give us the ultimate victory over sin.

We have this assurance from God's Word: "This is the victory that has overcome the world—our faith" (1 John 5:4). If you are a Christian, then you are "freed from sin" (Rom. 6:7). Sin has no more power over your life today than you allow it to have. What lie have you bought into that is causing you to panic? Choose today to believe God's truth: "If God is for us, who is against us?" (8:31).

Third, *God promised that Israel would divide the land as an inheritance.* The Lord said to Joshua, "You shall give this people possession of the land which I swore to their fathers to give them" (Josh. 1:6). This promise reaches far back into Israel's history to the time when Abraham (then called Abram) left his home in Ur and headed west, traveling to a land that God had promised to him. When Abraham passed through the land, the Lord appeared to him there and said, "To your descendants I will give this land" (Gen. 12:6–7).

As Christians, we have God's promise to give us an inheritance that is different from a plot of real estate on earth but rather is "an inheritance which is imperishable and undefiled and will not fade away, reserved in heaven for you" (1 Pet. 1:4). Because God always keeps His promises, we can take courage no matter what circumstances we encounter here on earth, because we know that our eternal inheritance in heaven is secure.

At the end of his life, Joshua reminded the people of God's faithfulness. In Joshua 23:14, he said, "Not one word of all the good words which the LORD your God spoke concerning you has failed; all have been fulfilled for you, not one of them has failed." God kept all His promises to Joshua, and He will keep all His promises to you and me. However, before God fulfills His promises to us, we have to exercise our faith.

Courage from God's Word

When we encounter situations that tempt us to panic, we can take courage not only in God but also in God's Word. Joshua faced a physical enemy: the giants who occupied the land. Few of us will ever have to cross swords with another human being, but all of us will have to cross swords with evil and its devastating effects. If we are going to win this invisible—but very real—war, we must follow God's instructions completely.

Joshua had to make the same commitment. The Lord told him that to succeed, Joshua had to take care "to do according to all the law which Moses My servant commanded" (Josh. 1:7). Let's look at the three commitments that required.

First, *Joshua was to walk a straight line.* The Lord said to Joshua, "Do not turn from [Moses's instructions] to the right or to the left" (v. 7). I often say—well, to be honest, I yell—something similar to drivers on the Dallas freeways: "Keep it between the lines!" Joshua was not to deviate one iota from God's instructions. Likewise, we must be careful to walk according to the teaching and example of our Lord Jesus Christ, without veering into the "broad" path that "leads to destruction" (Matt. 7:13). As Jesus explained, "The gate is small and the way is narrow that leads to life, and there are few who find it" (v. 14).

Second, *Joshua was to speak the truth*. The Lord told Joshua, "This book of the law shall not depart from your mouth" (Josh. 1:8). The taste of truth was to remain on his tongue. The only way Joshua could accomplish this was by consuming the Word of God through regular reading, study, and application.

We too have been given the responsibility to speak the truth. Ephesians 4:15 says, "Speaking the truth in love, we are to grow up in all aspects into Him who is the head, even Christ." We are called to know God's truth and then to stand for the truth whenever God's Word is being maligned. Now, it's important to remember that this verse says, "speaking the truth *in love*." When we stand for truth, some people will be turned off by that. But many people have been turned off to Christianity not because of the offense of the gospel but because of the offensiveness of other Christians. We need to speak the truth, but we need to speak it in love.

Third, *Joshua was to think biblical thoughts*. Referring to the book of the law, the Lord said, "You shall meditate on it day and night" (Josh. 1:8). Joshua was to memorize Scripture and repeat it over and over in his thoughts. The Hebrew word for "meditate" means to turn over, to moan, or to mutter. Joshua was to be so preoccupied with God's Word that he muttered passages of Scripture as he went about his daily routines. As we will examine further in chapter 5, one of the most effective ways to overcome our fears and move forward in faith is by committing Scripture to memory.

Faithfulness to these three commands equips us, like Joshua, "to do . . . all that is written" in God's Word (v. 8). Only then will we be able to fulfill God's calling on our lives and "have success" (v. 8).

Courage from God's Presence

Whenever our circumstances tempt us to panic, we can draw courage from God's promises and God's Word. But God has one more assurance for us: His presence.

In Joshua 1:9, God said to Joshua, "The LORD your God is with you wherever you go." And because that was true, the Lord commanded him, "Be strong and courageous! Do not tremble or be dismayed" (v. 9). Yes, Joshua would face giants and fortified cities, but he had nothing to fear because God Himself would be with him.

Throughout the Bible, we find reminder after reminder of God's unceasing presence. Perhaps one of the most beautiful is recorded in the Old Testament book of Isaiah. Speaking through the prophet, God promised, "Do not fear, for I am with you; do not anxiously look about you, for I am your God. I will strengthen you, surely I will help you, surely I will uphold you with My righteous right hand" (Isa. 41:10).

No matter what happens, God is with us. What a great comfort and source of courage is the presence of our Lord!

Be Brave

When life feels out of control, God's words are not pretty-sounding platitudes meant to make us feel better. God is not like a kindly old grandfather who absentmindedly pats our heads and says, "There, there. Everything will be okay." No, when God gives us a promise, He speaks with the authority of the Creator of the universe, who not only brought the world into existence by the power of His Word but also continues to speak to us today.

So, when God commanded Joshua to "be strong and courageous" (Josh. 1:6–7, 9), Israel's new leader was able to respond with obedience. I think it's interesting to note the order of the words in this command, because only when we are strong are we able to be courageous. The Hebrew word for "strong" (*hazaq*) refers to internal confidence. Only after Joshua developed his inner strength by relying on God's promises, God's Word, and God's presence could he then be "courageous" (*'amets*), which is the external quality of boldness. Courage is confidence in action.

The key to having courage during difficult times is facing your fears in faith. Before you go to bed tonight, I encourage you to make a list of the three things that frighten you the most. Are you fearful of what is happening in our nation's cultural climate? Are you worried about international unrest—rogue nations with nuclear bombs or terrorists? Or are your fears closer to home: the illness of a loved one, a rebellious child, the suspicion that your spouse is having an affair, a downturn in your business, or the loss of a job?

Make your list. Then, with the help of a Bible concordance or a godly friend, find at least one Scripture reference to write down next to each concern. For example, are you fearful that you won't be able to provide for yourself and your family financially? Next to that specific fear, write out Matthew 6:25–26:

> For this reason I say to you, do not be worried about your life, as to what you will eat or what you will drink; nor for your body, as to what you will put on. Is not life more than

food, and the body more than clothing? Look at the birds of the air, that they do not sow, nor reap nor gather into barns, and yet your heavenly Father feeds them. Are you not worth much more than they?

Claim those passages as God's promises for you. Memorize those verses and then meditate on them every time you are tempted to panic. In time, the Lord will build up your confidence so that you can live with courage.

No Reason for Panic

To give in to fear is to assume that you are powerless. And in many instances, you and I *are* powerless. We are probably powerless to stop terrorism or to cure cancer, for example. But if we allow our fears to morph into panic, then we are assuming God is also powerless—and we know He is anything but that! In the words of Peter Kreeft, "God had more power in one breath of his spirit than all the winds of war, all the nuclear bombs, all the energy of all the suns in all the galaxies, all the fury of Hell itself."[9] So why should we "tremble or be dismayed" (Josh. 1:9)?

This week I read Mark Batterson's book *All In*. In it he tells the story of a group of missionaries who a century ago were known as "one-way missionaries," so called because they only bought one-way tickets to the mission field. In fact, they didn't pack suitcases; they packed their belongings in coffins because they intended to be buried in foreign lands. One of these missionaries was A. W. Milne, who set sail for the New Hebrides Islands in the South Pacific. Tribesmen had martyred every missionary to these islands. And yet Milne packed his coffin and boarded a ship. He wasn't afraid of death. He had already died—to himself. If he lost his life in the endeavor, he would do so knowing that he had been faithful to Christ, who called him to minister among these South Pacific tribespeople.

Expecting a martyr's death that never came, Milne ministered in New Hebrides for thirty-five years. When the Lord eventually took His servant home, the tribespeople buried Milne in the coffin he had brought and erected a tombstone. This was the epitaph they carved on it: "When he came, there was no light. When he died, there was no darkness."[10]

What was it that gave Milne the courage to face death and live among those who had killed other missionaries who had come to their islands? He relied on Jesus's promise: "Do not fear what you are about to suffer. . . . Be faithful until death, and I will give you the crown of life" (Rev. 2:10). And he relied on Jesus's presence: "I will never desert you, nor will I ever forsake you" (Heb. 13:5).

The promise and presence of Jesus kept Milne from panic. And it will do the same for you. No matter what distress you might be experiencing right now, there is no reason to panic. As Paul wrote, "God has not given us a spirit of timidity, but of power and love and discipline" (2 Tim. 1:7). Whenever you are tempted to become anxious about the shifts taking place in our culture or the turbulence in your own life, you can take courage in this unchanging promise: "Greater is He who is in you than he who is in the world" (1 John 4:4).

Gain Situational Awareness

In the early hours of June 30, 2013, forty-three-year-old Eric Marsh, superintendent of the Granite Mountain Hotshots, emerged from his sleeping bag at Fire Station 7 in Prescott, Arizona. He brewed a pot of coffee, which he drank black. "There's no milk or sugar on the fire line, so why get used to it any other way?" he would say.

Carrying his steaming mug, Marsh walked into the ready room, where his tight-knit team of wildland firefighters met every morning. Tacked on the wall behind him was a poster that featured devastating pictures of wildfire fatalities, in which skilled firefighters had been caught off guard while battling small wildfires that escalated unexpectedly. In ominously large letters, the poster asked, "How is your situational awareness today?"[1]

By 5:15 a.m., most of the crew had gathered in the ready room. "We've got an assignment to Yarnell," Marsh said. "It's three hundred acres and burning on a ridgetop in thick chaparral. It's going to be hot—real hot." By 5:40, Marsh and his crew of nineteen firefighters—"his kids," as he referred to them—loaded their two fire trucks and headed toward the small town of Yarnell, about an hour south of Prescott.

Once on the fire line, Marsh set his team to work while he scouted out the fire. Noticing a shift in the weather, he sent one of his firefighters back down the mountain to serve as a lookout in case the fire pivoted. It did. The firebreak they had been cutting was suddenly compromised, so Marsh and his remaining eighteen crew members had to retreat. The radio crackled, asking if the Granite Mountain Hotshots were okay. They were. They had reached the black—an island of ash that the fire had left the day before. The brush had already been incinerated, robbing the fire of fuel, making it the safest place to be.

Then the fire pivoted again and raced downhill toward Yarnell, threatening homes and ranches. Marsh decided to leave the black in hopes of saving some of the homes. "He couldn't have imagined that, by heading for town, he was leading his crew toward a series of increasingly compromised circumstances, each more desperate than the last," one reporter wrote.

As the firefighters hiked down the mountain, the raging wildfire became obscured by a ridgeline. Without eyes on the fire, Marsh had a decision to make: bail off to his right and head for the safety of the desert floor two thousand feet below, or continue toward Yarnell in hopes of saving homes. He decided to continue toward Yarnell.

Descending an additional five hundred feet through thick chaparral, Marsh and his team found themselves in a basin, walled in on three sides by granite boulders. This was an extremely dangerous place, because it offered no means of escape. Just then the worst happened: they heard the roar of flames that had been obscured by the ridgeline. Through the smoke, Marsh saw the fire ripping up the hill toward them. They were trapped.

Eric Marsh and all eighteen of the firefighters with him died in that basin—the most wildland firefighters ever killed in a single incident. Their bodies were found under fire shelters—small aluminum tents meant to protect firefighters from extreme heat, but not from direct flames. The fire had burned over them so quickly and with such intensity that the massive granite walls of the basin cracked like eggshells.

After the fire, Marty Cole, a friend of Eric Marsh and the safety officer on the Yarnell Hill Fire, stood among the charred bodies of the Granite Mountain Hotshots. *What were they doing here?* Marty thought. Eric was too good a wildland firefighter to have led his team into this situation. Yet he did.

Gain Situational Awareness

You and I will likely never experience the inferno of a three-hundred-acre brushfire, as Eric Marsh and his Granite Mountain Hotshots did that day. But at some point in our lives, we will experience personal trials that seem to burn just as hot. Many of us have been burned when we lost something forever, such as a broken relationship that will never mend due to death or divorce, a missed opportunity that we can never regain, or a reputation that has been permanently charred by lies and bad decisions. Others have been singed

41

by personal sins that still smolder or by a scalding sense of loneliness and despair. We all have burn marks that scar our lives. All of us smell of smoke.

Not only that, but as believers in Jesus Christ, you and I are trapped—seemingly with no escape—in the cultural brushfires that threaten to consume everything that is godly in our society. The surging flames of secularism have exploded over our cultural landscape with such intensity that they have left our nation's biblical foundation cracked like eggshells.

Without a doubt, our world today is far removed from the teachings of Jesus. If we are to have any hope of surviving as Christians in the twenty-first century, it's not enough for us simply to talk about things that we could do better. We need practical, biblical steps to guide us away from ungodliness and toward righteousness.

Learn to Deny Denial

The question that hung over Eric Marsh's shoulder in the Granite Mountain Hotshots' ready room that Sunday morning is a haunting one: How is your situational awareness today? This question is not just for wildfire fighters. Ask any disaster survivor or first responder, and they will tell you that as soon as your circumstances turn dangerous, the first thing you must do—after you've composed yourself and taken courage—is gain situational awareness. As quickly as possible, you must ascertain the truth about your circumstances.

"Wait a minute," you may be saying. "Whenever I'm going through a difficult situation, I obviously know what's going on." Although you and I tend to *think* we know what is happening around us, the reality is that most people's immediate reaction in survival situations is to pretend things aren't as bad as they appear to be. Our minds tend to play tricks on us, causing us to misread the reality of our situation.

Not long ago, I remember watching news reports that described a tragic example of this kind of denial. Several years ago I received a call from Fox News asking me to come on the air immediately to comment on the tragic massacre that occurred in Las Vegas when a madman began opening fire on a large crowd at an outdoor country music festival. Many concertgoers thought they heard fireworks—even though there were no visible explosions in the sky and people around them were falling to the ground wounded or dead.[2] They understandably wanted to deny what they were witnessing with their own eyes.

If I had attended that concert, I probably would have assumed the sound was fireworks as well. Average people like me aren't used to the sound of gunfire. So, at the crack of a gun, we tend to disbelieve our ears. Our minds try to make sense of what is taking place by substituting a dangerous and unfamiliar sound (gunfire) with a safe and familiar sound (fireworks).

We see this kind of substitution all the time in our contemporary culture. For example, when we read about the rise of cyberbullying and online harassment among today's adolescents, we tend to dismiss it as typical teenage behavior. When we observe attempts to take away Christians' First Amendment rights, we shrug and say it's just the way things are now. And when we hear pastors and celebrities say that we shouldn't judge people's beliefs since "all religions

43

lead to heaven," we decide they are being compassionate and tolerant.

But survivors learn to see and call things as they truly are, not as they wish them to be. That's why people who had developed the skill of gaining situational awareness—such as the combat veterans and police officers who were at the 2017 Las Vegas country music festival—immediately realized the truth of what was taking place: someone was shooting into the crowd. The only question was from where.

Correctly Assess Reality

Perhaps at no other time in history has there been a greater need to be aware of what is taking place around us. If you and I are going to survive—and thrive—in our ever-changing culture, we too need to learn how to gain situational awareness. And for us to correctly assess reality, we need wisdom.

In our current day, the wisdom to accurately gauge reality seems to be in short supply. For example, at no other time in human history have we been so confused about the nature of male and female. Academics, entertainers, and politicians tell us that we live in the age of gender fluidity— that we are no longer a society where boys are boys and girls are girls.[3]

And gender isn't the only thing that is fluid these days. It seems that our ethnicity is something we can choose to change as well. A growing number of people identify as trans-racial—in other words, Caucasians who perceive themselves as African Americans, Pacific Islanders identifying as Native Americans, and so on.[4] Believe it or not, even our age may no longer be set in stone. Not long ago, I read of a sixty-nine-year-old Dutch businessman who claimed discrimination by a dating website and launched a court battle to legally identify as twenty years younger.[5] And in perhaps the most bizarre case of incorrectly assessing reality, a growing number of people, called "otherkin," identify as something other than human![6]

Whenever I hear things like this, I recall God's warning in Isaiah 5:20: "Woe to those who call evil good, and good evil; who substitute darkness for light and light for darkness; who substitute bitter for sweet and sweet for bitter!" This is a divine denunciation against those who mock what God calls good and evil. But God has the last word on the matter. Galatians 6:7 says, "God is not mocked; for whatever a man sows, this he will also reap."

As our society increasingly considers evil to be good and sees biblical morality as deviant, it is imperative for Christians to have the courage to be aware—and stay aware—of what is going on around us.

Our Present Last Days

More than two thousand years ago, the apostle Paul warned of this coming moral decline. In 2 Timothy 3:1, he gave this flashing caution sign: "Realize this, that in the last days difficult times will come." Paul was saying, "You'd better buckle up and get ready, because the last days are going to be terrible times." As I wrote in my book *Countdown to the Apocalypse*, "Don't be naive and think it's all going to be okay. It's not all going to be okay. But forewarned is forearmed.

If we know what is going to happen, we won't be surprised when it does."[7]

What did Paul mean by "last days"? Recently, I was preaching to a large group on the top of the Mount of Olives in Jerusalem—the location of both Christ's ascension into heaven as well as His return to earth one day. As soon as Jesus ascended into heaven, the clock started ticking toward the date of Jesus's second coming. Although no one knows exactly where we are on God's timeline of the end times, we do know that the countdown to Christ's return has begun. So in that sense, we are currently living in the last days as we await the return of Jesus Christ. And as the years, months, and days lead up to His return, things on earth are going to get worse.

Notice that Paul described these present last days as "difficult." This Greek word occurs only one other time in the New Testament—in Matthew 8:28, where it depicts two demon-possessed men as "extremely violent." You could translate this phrase as "times without moral restraint." Just as those demon-possessed men had no restraint and committed unspeakable acts, so it will be in the last days.

If we are to survive what is going on in our nation, our classrooms, and our own homes and hearts in these present last days, then we must pay close attention to what is happening around us. That's what Paul meant when he said, "Let us be alert and sober" (1 Thess. 5:6). And that is why I heed this sage advice from theologian Karl Barth: "Take your Bible and take your newspaper [or your Facebook newsfeed], and read both. But interpret newspapers from your Bible."[8] The newspaper tells us what is happening in the world, and the Bible tells us what it means.

The Descendants of Issachar: "Men Who Understood the Times"

You and I can gain wisdom about the world we live in from a little-known but profound verse that is buried in an Old Testament list of names. On the surface, this verse doesn't look like much. But when we dig a little deeper, we uncover a profound treasure.

> Of the sons of Issachar, *men who understood the times, with knowledge of what Israel should do*, their chiefs were two hundred; and all their kinsmen were at their command. (1 Chron. 12:32)

To appreciate what this verse is teaching, we need some background. Issachar was the ninth son of Jacob. Just before Jacob died, he blessed Issachar, calling him "a strong donkey" (hardly a compliment in our day, but trust me, it was in Jacob's day!) and foreseeing that he would find rest in a pleasant land. Then Jacob shared these words about his son's future: "When he saw that a resting place was good and that the land was pleasant, [Issachar] bowed his shoulder to bear burdens, and became a slave at forced labor" (Gen. 49:15).

When Jacob's descendants—the Israelites—left Egypt, conquered the promised land, and then divided the territory among the twelve tribes, Issachar's portion was a small but fertile tract between the Kishon and Jordan Rivers. As Jacob had predicted, it was a pleasant land, some of the most fruitful in Israel. So Issachar's descendants became farmers, cultivating the ground to produce fruits, vegetables, and nuts.

Today, few of us are familiar with the rigors of farming. I have lived most of my life in major cities, where my food supply comes primarily from the local supermarket. But I will never forget the years I pastored a wonderful church in the rural town of Eastland, Texas, where I had the opportunity to observe farm life firsthand. My friends who worked as ranchers and farmers consistently got up before sunrise and endured long hours of physically demanding labor as they tended to their land and cattle. They carefully studied the seasons, followed the weather patterns, and watched for any signs of insects or illness.

Like my farming friends in Eastland, the descendants of Issachar were also keen observers of the natural world. They examined the soil, learned how to guard against insects and blights, observed the weather, and studied seasonal patterns to know the best times for planting and harvesting. After generations of mastering the skills of observation, correlation, and application, it's no wonder the descendants of Issachar "understood the times, with knowledge of what Israel should do" (1 Chron. 12:32).

The Hebrew word for "understood" in this verse means discernment, insight, or wisdom. The descendants of Issachar understood not only the physical climate but were aware of their current cultural and political climate as well. And as a result, they were able to discern the times.

When they sensed unrest among the people, they surmised it was time for David to expand his kingdom. They correctly perceived what was taking place and were able to take the right course of action, which was to establish David as king over Israel.

You might be saying, "This biblical background is interesting, but what does it have to do with my life today?" Well, it means that you and I need to become descendants of Issachar in our own times. Put in survivalist terms, we need to gain situational awareness—the wisdom to understand what is taking place in our culture, our homes, and our hearts—so that we too will know the right actions to take.

Growing in Wisdom

Unfortunately, the wisdom obtained by the descendants of Issachar wasn't automatically passed down in our DNA. If it were, I would never have made a fool of myself at an airport a few years ago. As I was waiting for my flight number to be called, I decided to make one final stop at the restroom before boarding the plane. While I was washing my hands, I noticed a woman entering the restroom. She stopped when she saw me and apologized profusely for being in the wrong restroom. "Don't worry about it," I said. "It happens all the time." Clearly embarrassed, she darted out of there. I dried my hands and straightened my tie.

As I left the restroom, for some reason I happened to look back. Posted on the wall next to the entrance was a feminine stick figure with the word *Women* underneath it. I had been the one in the wrong restroom the whole time! I definitely should have practiced more situational awareness that day!

Situational awareness requires wisdom—and, fortunately for me, wisdom is a skill that we can acquire. How do we obtain the wisdom of Issachar's descendants? The Bible tells us that there are three primary ways we can gain and grow in wisdom.

① *Have the Proper Attitude*

First, if we want to acquire wisdom, we must have the proper attitude toward God. In Proverbs 9:10, the wisest man who ever lived, King Solomon, reveals the foundation upon which a life of wisdom is built: "The fear of the LORD is the beginning of wisdom."

This proverb presumes two things: first, that God exists, and second, that He is the source of wisdom. The truth is, no matter how many academic degrees we may have, you and I can find real wisdom only through a relationship with God in which we fear Him—not in dread but in awe and obedience. To fear God means to have a healthy respect for God's power and a reverence for God's holiness that results in the reordering of our behavior.

When God gave the law to govern the lives of the Israelites, the first commandment concerned their relationship with Him. Exodus 20:3 says, "You shall have no other gods before Me." And when Jesus was asked to identify the greatest commandment, He said it was, "You shall love the Lord your God with all your heart, and with all your soul, and with all your mind" (Matt. 22:37).

Jesus demonstrated His love and fear of God throughout His life. When He confronted the Pharisees after healing a man on the Sabbath, He told them, "I do not seek My own will, but the will of Him who sent Me" (John 5:30). Even at the greatest crisis of His life, Jesus maintained His love and fear of God. In the Garden of Gethsemane, when He struggled in prayer before His arrest and execution, Jesus said, "Yet not My will, but Yours be done" (Luke 22:42).

You and I can become wise by following the way of wisdom, which is the way of Jesus Christ. It all begins with choosing to have the proper attitude toward God—making Him the center of our lives.

Actively Search for Wisdom

Second, if we want to grow in wisdom, we must actively seek to acquire wisdom. Throughout the book of Proverbs, we are encouraged to search diligently for wisdom as though searching for buried treasure. For example, Proverbs 2:4–5 says, "If you seek her [wisdom] as silver and search for her as for hidden treasures; then you will discern the fear of the LORD and discover the knowledge of God."

Exactly how do we go about searching for wisdom? I can think of at least three actions to accomplish this.

First, *look for wisdom*. The late businessman Fred Smith advised, "If you have a choice, always work for either the best or the worst boss, for from the good ones you learn what to do and from the bad ones you learn what not to do."[9] When I was the youth minister at First Baptist Dallas, I'll never forget what my pastor, Dr. W. A. Criswell, told me: "Someday, Robert, you will be the pastor of this church and you will have your own staff. If you want to know how to handle a staff, just watch what I do carefully, take notes, and then do the *opposite*, and you will be a success!" Dr. Criswell had many strengths, but he was terrible at overseeing staff members—and he knew it! I'm grateful for all Dr. Criswell taught me about what to do—and what not to do.

This same truth applies to gaining wisdom. In the book of Proverbs, Solomon urged us to look at the foolish to learn what to avoid and to look at the wise to learn what to embrace.

Second, *listen to those who are wise.* In the book of Proverbs, we can almost see Solomon walking the streets of Jerusalem or the surrounding fields, saying to his son, "See that?"—and then drawing some practical lesson about life. Throughout his writings, Solomon said, "Son, listen to the instructions of your father and the teaching of your mother" (Prov. 1:8; 6:20). If we want to be wise, we should listen to those who are wise.

Finally, if we want to find wisdom, we must *ask for wisdom.* James, the half-brother of Jesus, wrote, "You do not have because you do not ask" (James 4:2). There is a shortage of wisdom in our world today because too few Christians are asking for wisdom. James also wrote, "If any of you lacks wisdom, you should ask God, who gives generously to all without finding fault, and it will be given to you" (1:5 NIV). Wisdom isn't some abstract idea that we can never attain. Wisdom is God's point of view about our specific circumstances. Whenever we need God's perspective about things that are happening in our world—and in our lives—today, the Bible says all we have to do is ask.

Take Action

The third way to grow in wisdom is to apply what we learn. You and I can fear the Lord and search diligently for wisdom, but if we don't apply what we have discovered to our own lives, then we aren't being wise; we are being foolish. Without exercising application, all the understanding and knowledge in the world are merely intellectual gymnastics—interesting to watch, perhaps, but not effective in making lasting change.

When we choose to watch from a distance and simply pontificate about what is taking place in our culture and our own circumstances, without taking any actions to apply what we have learned, we are not being wise. Daniel 11:32 says that "the people who know their God will display strength and *take action*."

Gaining—and Maintaining—Situational Awareness

I wish I could promise you that there will be a time in your life when you can relax and say, "I've obtained all the wisdom I need for the rest of my life!" But the search for wisdom is a lifelong pursuit. Why? Because the battle we face with our Enemy is a lifelong struggle.

Every day, we clash with a world system that is increasingly hostile to God, the corrupting temptations of our flesh, or the devil himself, who desires to derail us from our devotion to Jesus. At no point can we let down our guard. If we do, then like Eric Marsh and his Granite Mountain Hotshots, who were caught off guard by the approaching flames, we will be burned.

In 1 Thessalonians 5, the apostle Paul commended the early believers for their understanding of the times: "As to the times and the epochs, brethren, you have no need of anything to be written to you. For you yourselves know full well" (vv. 1–2). He then urged these believers to continue to stay aware of their current events in light of biblical truth: "Let us not sleep as others do, but let us be alert and sober" (v. 6).

This verse gives us three practical steps for maintaining the situational awareness that God's wisdom provides.

4. Stay Awake

First, Paul said, "Let us not sleep" (v. 6). The metaphor of sleeping in this context doesn't refer to death but to an unawareness of the times. In other words, Paul was saying, "Don't sleepwalk through life, unaware of what is happening in the world around you."

This biblical principle of staying awake and not falling asleep reminds me of a story from my childhood. When my younger brother, Tim, and I were growing up, we used to get into horrible fights with each other. The main source of our conflict was our shared bathroom, which connected our bedrooms. Tim had this annoying habit. When he finished in the bathroom he always forgot to unlock the door on my side. I would try to go to the restroom, jiggle the doorknob, and find it locked. So I'd have to stomp around through the hall into his bedroom and go in that way.

One night, I came home late and needed to go to the restroom. I jiggled the door; it was locked again. Well, I'd had it. A few weeks earlier, I had gone to a magic shop in downtown Dallas and purchased a vial of stink perfume. It looked like real perfume until you opened it. It had the most putrid smell you can imagine. I was so mad that night that I got my vial of stink perfume and crept into Tim's bedroom, where he was asleep. I opened that vial of perfume and poured it all out on his pillow. He woke up and bolted out of the bed!

Now, that's a humorous illustration of the need to stay alert and on guard against attacks from our enemies—or, in this case, our sibling. But the principle of staying aware of our situation is very real. We can't hide our heads in the sand. We can't pretend that we can cloister in our holy huddles and let the world pass us by. The devil has your scent and "prowls around like a roaring lion, seeking someone to devour" (1 Pet. 5:8). So snap out of your slumber. Wake up and "be very careful, then, how you live—not as unwise but as wise, making the most of every opportunity, because the days are evil" (Eph. 5:15–16 NIV).

 ### Stay Hopeful

Paul also told believers to "be alert" (1 Thess. 5:6). Throughout the Bible, we are instructed to stay alert. In Luke 21:36, Jesus told His disciples to "keep on the alert at all times." And Peter wrote, "Be on the alert" (1 Pet. 5:8).

When it comes to what is happening in our nation and in our families, we need to call things as they really are. It is true that we are living in the last days, but it is equally true that God sits on the throne and rules. Nothing catches Him off guard, because, as Psalm 121:4 reminds us, "He who keeps Israel will neither slumber nor sleep." No matter how hopeless our current situation may seem, we can be confident that "nothing is too difficult for [Him]" (Jer. 32:17).

So as you keep an eye on your situation, remember to keep things in proper perspective. You and I do not have to fear when things appear to be out of control, because we know the One who is in control. And we can rest assured that "God causes all things to work together for good to those who love God, to those who are called according to His purpose" (Rom. 8:28).

6 *Stay Serious*

Finally, Paul commanded us to be "sober" (1 Thess. 5:6). This is exactly what Peter wrote in 1 Peter 5:8: "Be of sober spirit." When it comes to being aware of our current situation, being "sober" means being self-controlled in our personal lives.

We don't have to go through life as if we were weaned on a dill pickle, but we do need to be serious-minded, not frivolous. Why is this important to gaining situational awareness? Speaking to His disciples about the events that would take place before His second coming, Jesus said, "Be on guard, so that your hearts will not be weighted down with dissipation and drunkenness and the worries of life" (Luke 21:34). Jesus was saying that self-indulgence and the cares of everyday life can blind us to what is taking place around us. We need to be on guard and self-controlled to assess our circumstances accurately.

Vice President Mike Pence recently delivered a message to graduates at Liberty University that, if I were to title it, would be called "Gain Situational Awareness." Here's what he said:

> You know, throughout most of American history, it's been pretty easy to call yourself a Christian. It didn't even occur to people that you might be shunned or ridiculed for defending the teaching of the Bible.
>
> But thing are different now. Some of the loudest voices for tolerance today have little tolerance for traditional Christian beliefs. So as you go about your daily life, just be ready. Because you're going to be asked not just to tolerate things that violate your faith; you're going to be asked to endorse

them. You're going to be asked to bow down to the idols of the popular culture.

So you need to prepare your minds for action. . . . You need to show that we can love God and love our neighbor at the same time through words and deeds. And you need to be prepared to meet opposition.

As the founder of this university often said, "No one ever achieved greatness without experiencing opposition."

So . . . as you strive for greatness, know that you'll face challenges, you'll face opposition. But just know this: If, like Shadrach, Meshach, and Abednego, you end up in the fire, there'll be another in the fire.[10]

He was telling these students to stay awake, stay hopeful, and stay serious. If they—and we—can do that, then we will walk in the way of wisdom and gain the situational awareness essential to living courageously in this hostile world.

Take Inventory

By 1970, public interest in crewed space flight was declining rapidly. The exciting days of the space race to determine who would dominate the cosmos—the United States or the Soviet Union—were over. When American astronaut Neil Armstrong put the first human footprint on the moon on July 21, 1969, the United States claimed victory over space.

So when NASA launched its third moon mission nine months later, it was met with a collective yawn by the American public. But an explosion on *Apollo 13* two days into their flight changed all that.

Jack Swigert, the command module pilot, flipped a switch to turn on the fans as part of a routine "cryo stir" in the hydrogen tanks. Sixteen seconds later, he was startled by a large boom. Warning lights flashed and alarms sounded in the command module as the ship began to shudder. Oxygen pressure and power levels plummeted. Swigert radioed, "Houston, we've had a problem."[1]

Within a matter of minutes, the *Odyssey*, the lifeboat for the three American astronauts, was dying. Mission control in Houston determined the astronauts had to shut down the *Odyssey* and move into the undamaged lunar lander, the *Aquarius*. Once there, the crew would perform a number of maneuvers to slingshot themselves around the moon—using the moon's gravitational pull to gain additional energy—and head back to earth. To save precious power, several systems in the *Aquarius* had to be shut down.

The lunar lander was designed to carry two people for no more than thirty-six hours. However, with the command module blacked out, all three astronauts would have to survive the trip back to earth in the cramped confines of *Aquarius*. It would take the spacecraft ninety-six hours to make the return trip home.

It didn't take long for the astronauts to notice that the lunar lander was filling with dangerously high levels of carbon dioxide (CO_2), since its scrubber was unable to filter out the poisonous gas expelled by the three men. On their trip to and around the moon, the astronauts had replaced the filter at least twice. As they emerged from the dark side of the moon, they had one filter left, but it came from the command module and wouldn't fit the lunar lander's compartment. Built by two different contractors, the command module's CO_2 filter was square while the lunar lander's filter was round.

To keep the three men from dying of asphyxiation, a team in Houston gathered an inventory of equipment the astronauts had on board and began piecing together a contraption to fit the proverbial square peg into a round hole. The inventory consisted of the square lithium-hydroxide canister,

Adapt, improvise, overcome

a roll of duct tape, two plastic bags, two hoses from moon suits, two socks, the cover of the flight plan, and a bungee cord to secure the modified filtration system to *Aquarius*'s bulkhead.

As the 1995 movie *Apollo 13* dramatically depicted, the "mailbox," as the contraption was called, worked. The astronauts safely splashed down in the Pacific Ocean and were welcomed home—the heroes of NASA's most successful failure.

Take Inventory

The survival of the *Apollo 13* astronauts depended entirely on the ingenuity of technicians and engineers in Houston who worked from the inventory of supplies available to the astronauts in space. For example, it would have done no good to instruct the astronauts to tie the plastic bag around one of the hoses if there was no bungee cord on board the spaceship. The success of the "mailbox" depended on what the astronauts could do with the inventory on hand.

This is true in every survival situation. In this book, we have been looking at strategies to survive the troubles we encounter in our culture and in our lives. Our first survival tip is *don't panic.* No matter what the situation may be, take a deep breath, remain calm, and remember that God is in control. The second survival tip we looked at is *gain situational awareness.* As quickly as possible, pay attention to your circumstances and call things as they truly are, not as you wish them to be.

Once you've gotten your wits about you and have gained some sense of what is happening, the next step is to take an inventory of your equipment—of what you have or what you can find around you. For survivalists, the difference between life and death, in many cases, is as simple as a map and compass, a knife and fork, or even a shoelace.

I realize that I'm showing my age here, but I remember watching a television show in the 1980s that was a great example of finding and creatively using pieces of this-and-that. I was intrigued by the way Angus MacGyver, the hero of the hit show *MacGyver*, could use nothing but a paper clip, chocolate milk, or a pair of binoculars to disarm a missile, create an explosive device, or divert a dangerous laser beam. He was a master of bricolage—the skill of building useful things from whatever is at hand. MacGyver was able to use any tool that was available in any given situation to save the world.

Of course, the chances are slim that you and I are ever going to be a MacGyver who saves the day in a life-or-death situation. But in a way, we are called on every day to be a MacGyver to our families, our churches, and our communities. As Christians, we are to use the tools we have available to serve God and help others. Fortunately, God has given us an extensive inventory of tools that we can use not only to navigate our challenging times but also to fulfill His calling in our lives.

The Armor of God

Now, when it comes to taking inventory in your current situation, I've got some good news and some bad news. The bad news is that Satan is a formidable opponent and wants to *armor of God*

destroy you. He is not going to rest until he does. But here's the good news: God has given you all the tools you need to defeat the devil's plan to destroy you. The Bible refers to those tools as "armor." That's why Ephesians 6:13 says, "Take up the full armor of God, so that you will be able to resist in the evil day, and having done everything, to stand firm." No matter what circumstances you may be facing right now, when you take inventory, you can be assured that God has supplied you with everything you need for victory.

Satan is the ultimate force behind many of the difficulties you and I face every day. Though people today may dismiss or even ridicule the notion of satanic attack, the Bible never does. The apostle Paul couldn't have been clearer about this when he wrote, "Our struggle is not against flesh and blood, but against the rulers, against the powers, against the world forces of this darkness, against the spiritual forces of wickedness in the heavenly places" (v. 12).

In other words, our real-world effects often have other-world causes. We tend to blame other people for our problems. We might say, "My struggle is with my spouse, who doesn't appreciate me," or "My struggle is against my boss, who mistreats me," or "My struggle is against my friend, who has wronged me." But Paul said, "No, our greatest obstacle in life is not another flesh-and-blood person. It is a spiritual power being used against us by a very real being that the Bible refers to as Satan."

The Bible is clear that Satan is the enemy of God and of God's people. Jesus called the devil "a murderer" and "a liar and the father of lies" (John 8:44). In 1 John 3:8, John said, "The devil has sinned from the beginning." And Peter told us to be spiritually serious and vigilant, because our "adversary, the devil, prowls around like a roaring lion, seeking someone to devour" (1 Pet. 5:8).

Satan is not only real but he has a scheme to destroy you. I don't use that term *scheme* accidentally. Ephesians 6:11 warns us to "Put on the full armor of God, so that you will be able to stand firm against the schemes of the devil." The word *schemes* (*methodia* in Greek) was originally used to describe a wild animal that would methodically stalk and then suddenly attack its victim. The predator would not treat all its prey in the same way. Different prey required different strategies.

In the same way, Satan has a unique "blueprint" that details his elaborate plan to destroy everything important to you.

Satan has a plan to destroy your marriage.

Satan has a plan for the rebellion of your children.

Satan has a plan to ensure your departure from the Christian faith.

Famous pastor David Martyn Lloyd-Jones warned of the danger of failing to recognize the spiritual battle being waged against us every minute of our lives: "Anyone who is not aware of a fight and a conflict in a spiritual sense is in a drugged and hazardous condition."[2] Remember, any lull you may be experiencing right now in Satan's attack on your life is only temporary—it's only time for him to reload and come at you again. If we are going to thrive as followers of Christ in this world, we must not be ignorant of Satan's schemes.

Someone has said, "Sin will take you further than you want to go, keep you longer than you want to stay, and cost more than you want to pay." Some have learned the hard way that all of Satan's promises are lies, yet they don't know how to find the truth. Others are deceived by Satan's lies and are willing to go wherever sin leads them. Both groups, however, have been "blinded . . . so that they might not see the light of the gospel of the glory of Christ, who is the image of God" (2 Cor. 4:4).

But there is hope! You and I don't have to be spiritual roadkill in this battle against Satan and his demons. We can prevail. This is the reason Paul urged believers, "Be strong in the Lord and in the strength of His might. Put on the full armor of God, so that you will be able to stand firm against the schemes of the devil" (Eph. 6:10–11).

When you and I put on the armor of God, we are strengthened by the supernatural power of Christ to defeat the supernatural forces of evil.

Our Spiritual Armor

Put on   *Belt shield sword shoe breastplate*

What is the "armor of God" that the Lord has provided for us? Using a Roman infantryman as his model, Paul mentioned five defensive pieces and one offensive piece. The purpose of this armor is to help us "resist [the devil and his evil schemes] in the evil day, and having done everything, to stand firm" (v. 13).

The original readers of Paul's letter would have immediately understood the analogy of armor, because Roman soldiers were a constant presence in their lives. If Paul were writing today, he might use a police officer's uniform as his example. My younger brother, Tim, was a lieutenant in the Dallas Police Department. Every time he went to work, he would carefully put on each item of the protective gear of his uniform: his badge, his gun and holster, and even his bulletproof vest. Each part of his uniform served an essential purpose in helping him carry out the job he had been assigned to do.

Likewise, each part of our spiritual "uniform" has an important purpose in equipping us for our spiritual struggles. Let's observe as Paul takes inventory of our spiritual weapons, in the order in which a Roman soldier would dress before going into battle.

Put On the Belt of Truth ①

Roman soldiers wore a free-flowing garment called a tunic. When they were going into combat, they put on a belt and then "girded [their] loins" (v. 14) by gathering the loose ends of the tunic from between their legs and tucking them into their belt. By keeping excess material from getting in the way, the soldier could move his legs quickly without constraint or fear of tripping.

Paul likened the soldier's belt to "truth" (v. 14). Just as a soldier would tighten his belt around his waist to secure his tunic during battle, so believers should buckle the Word of God around their minds. When thoughts come into our minds that tempt us to lust, anger, or fear, we need to immediately tuck those thoughts into the "belt" of God's Word so that they don't trip us up. We do this by recognizing those stray thoughts and replacing them with the truths of Scripture.

I think that is what Paul had in mind when he wrote, "For the weapons of our warfare are not of the flesh, but divinely powerful for the destruction of fortresses. We are destroying

66

speculations and every lofty thing raised up against the knowledge of God, and we are taking every thought captive to the obedience of Christ" (2 Cor. 10:4–5).

We can also defeat those distracting and destructive thoughts by following the example of the living Word of God—Jesus. In 1 Corinthians 11:1, Paul said to the Christians in Corinth, "Be imitators of me, just as I also am of Christ." When I read this verse, I can't help but think of the WWJD fad that was popular several decades ago. Do you remember it? Christians of all ages wore bracelets imprinted with WWJD—*What Would Jesus Do?*—reminding them to think about how Jesus might respond to a particular situation and to follow His example. We might not know what Jesus would do in every circumstance, or we might not always be able to do what He would do, but we will never go wrong if we try to follow Jesus's example.

Put On the Breastplate of Righteousness

The next piece of equipment a Roman soldier put on was a breastplate—a form-fitting metal shell that covered the soldier's upper body, front and back, held in place with leather straps. The purpose of the breastplate was to protect the soldier's spinal cord and vital organs.

Paul likened the breastplate to "righteousness" (Eph. 6:14). Now, *righteousness* is one of those terms we use in churches without really understanding what it means. I think we can safely say that Paul didn't have in mind self-righteousness—the belief that our good works alone will merit God's favor. How can I be sure that Paul didn't have this in mind? Take a look at Isaiah 64:6. Apart from God, Isaiah said, "All our righteous deeds are like a filthy garment." In the original Hebrew, the last phrase could be translated as "menstrual cloths." That is what God thinks of supposedly righteous deeds we perform in our own strength and for our own purposes.

"Righteousness" in the Bible usually refers to *imputed righteousness*. This is the right standing with God that we receive from Him as a gift when we trust in Jesus Christ as our Savior. The moment we become a Christian, when we confess our sins to God and receive His forgiveness, God performs a mysterious, twofold transaction. First, He takes our sin debt and credits, or imputes, it to Jesus's account. At the same time, He takes Jesus's righteousness and imputes it to our account. Here's how Paul described it in 2 Corinthians 5:21: "[God] made [Jesus] who knew no sin to be sin on our behalf, so that we might become the righteousness of God in Him."

In my book *The Divine Defense*, I described the results of this transaction: "While imputed righteousness assures us of escaping an eternity in hell, it does not exempt us from the attacks of Satan."[3] Therefore, in Ephesians 6 Paul must have been referring to another form of righteousness—what I call *practiced righteousness*. Another word for practiced righteousness is *obedience*. It is the moral behavior that comes from obeying God.

In 1 Timothy 6:11, Paul urged Timothy to flee unrighteous pursuits and instead "pursue righteousness, godliness, faith, love, perseverance and gentleness." A righteous or holy life—one trained through what the late Eugene Peterson called "a long obedience in the same direction"[4]—protects our hearts from Satan's attacks. When we are faithful to obey God's commands, we "do not give the devil an opportunity" in our lives (Eph. 4:27).

Lace Up the Boots of the Gospel

Well-made shoes were an essential part of a Roman soldier's armor. They wore sturdy sandals with thick soles and wide leather straps that covered their toes and the upper part of the foot. They were more like boots than modern sandals. The metal studs on the bottom of their shoes gave them increased traction in battle, like an athlete's cleats.

Paul compared the soldier's shoes to the gospel. He said, "Shod your feet with the preparation of the gospel of peace" (6:15). There is little doubt that Paul was referring to the good news of Jesus Christ, which is the only means of reconciliation—making peace—between a holy God and an unholy people. The spiritual boots in our armor refer to our willingness and ability to take the message of the gospel to others.

But Paul meant more than just delivering the good news to others. A soldier's boots also kept him from slipping in battle. In the same way, understanding our purpose in life— sharing the gospel with others—gives us stability in life, especially when Satan launches spiritual attacks against us.

Let me get personal for a moment. Whenever I'm tempted (and yes, pastors have to fight off temptation just like anybody else), the first thing I think about is this: If I give in to this temptation, and my sin is found out, how would it affect my family—my wife, my daughters, and my grandchildren? What would my sin do to the church I pastor and love? And how would it hurt the cause of Christ? My sin would give

69

the enemies of the Lord a reason to blaspheme, which is a strong motivation for me to stand firm when attacked.

And that's not just true of me; it's true for you too. If you are a Christian who has dedicated his or her life to sharing the good news of Jesus's death and resurrection with others, and you slip under an attack, it not only hurts you and your family personally but also hurts your witness for Christ.

But if you are a Christian who hasn't dedicated his or her life to sharing the gospel with others, maybe because you are afraid or just don't know how, let me encourage you: you can do it! Sharing God's message of salvation isn't difficult. In fact, a simple presentation of the gospel contains four essential truths.[5]

First, *all of us have sinned*. Every person has sinned and is guilty of breaking God's laws. Romans 3:23 says, "All have sinned and fall short of the glory of God." Although some people may break fewer laws than others, the reality is that we all fall short of God's standard of perfection.

Second, *we deserve to be punished for our sins*. Because we have disobeyed God's laws, we deserve to be punished for our disobedience. Romans 6:23 says, "The wages of sin is death." The word *death* refers not only to physical death but also to eternal separation from God in hell.

Third, *Christ died for our sins*. Jesus Christ willingly took the punishment that we deserve for our sins. Romans 5:8 says, "God demonstrates His own love toward us, in that while we were yet sinners, Christ died for us." The God whose holiness demands a payment for sin also made a way to pay the penalty for our sin through Jesus's death on the cross. Fourth, *we must receive God's gift of forgiveness.* A gift is not a gift unless it is received. John 1:12 says, "As many as received Him, to them He gave the right to become children of God, even to those who believe in His name." Salvation is a gift from God that must be received.

After sharing these four points, you can ask if the person understands what you have shared. If he or she indicates a desire to receive God's gift of forgiveness, then you can invite the person to repeat a prayer that goes something like this: "God, I know that I have sinned against You, and I am truly sorry for my sins. I believe that You sent Jesus to die on the cross to pay the penalty for me. Right now, I am trusting in Jesus to save me from my sins. Thank You for forgiving me. Help me to live for You. In Jesus's name I pray, amen."

Our preparation of the gospel will enable us to hold our ground against Satan's schemes. When disappointments, failures, and temptations threaten to push us around, our surefootedness on the truth of salvation will help us to be able to stand firm with peace in our hearts and minds.

Take Up the Shield of Faith

The next piece of armor in Paul's description was the shield. Roman shields were shaped like doors and offered full-body protection, measuring two-and-a-half feet wide and four feet long. Shield makers covered the thick wooden planks with canvas and then with calfskin. Metal strips were nailed to the tops and bottoms, and in the center was a metal protrusion designed to deflect arrows.

Paul likened a Christian's shield to "faith" (Eph. 6:16). What do we mean by faith? Hebrews 11:1 tells us, "Faith is the assurance of things hoped for, the conviction of things not seen." In other words, faith is being assured that God will do what He has promised to do and acting accordingly.

It is important for us to apply that trust at the moment of spiritual attack. To lay your shield aside—to go through life without faith—leaves you vulnerable to Satan's schemes, resulting in certain defeat. But resolute faith protects you from demonic attacks, rendering Satan's schemes useless.

How does the shield of faith do that? Paul said, "With [it] you will be able to extinguish all the flaming arrows of the evil one" (Eph. 6:16). Satan loves to send red-hot missiles into our lives. Sometimes the arrow is labeled *lust*. Sometimes the arrow is labeled *greed*. But I think one of his favorite arrows is *worry*—a paralyzing fear that seems to come out of nowhere into your life. And the reason I think this is one of Satan's favorite weapons is that worry has a way of stopping us in our tracks so we can't move forward in our relationship with God. Satan wants to get our mind centered on something that likely isn't going to happen and then paralyze us from making any progress in what God has planned for us.

Many years ago, while I was working in my church office, I was hit by an anxiety arrow that caused me to be overwhelmed by the thought I was going to die soon of some dreaded disease. There was some basis for the fear—both my parents died from cancer at a relatively young age. But I had no objective reason to believe I was ill. Nevertheless, I was so overcome with worry that I could not continue my work. Instead, I began calling doctor friends, describing my fears, my aches and pains, and my family history. Everyone was reassuring—except my insurance agent, who recommended I consider additional life insurance coverage. I wasted several hours of valuable time that afternoon because I did not raise my shield of faith.

Satan's attacks are meant to destroy reputations, families, and churches. But just as Roman soldiers soaked their shields in water to extinguish literal flaming arrows, so we should immerse ourselves in the things that will saturate our souls in faith: the Word of God and the people of God. All too often, we think we have to put on our spiritual armor and face the Enemy alone. Not so. Just as Roman soldiers held their shields together to create a wall in front while others placed their shields together above their heads to deflect arching arrows, so it is with us. Whenever we are besieged, we should call on our fellow soldiers to create a barrier around us.

Put On the Helmet of Salvation

The Roman helmet, like the helmets our military men and women wear today, was a vital piece of defensive equipment. Roman helmets were made of bronze and fitted over an iron skullcap lined with leather. Some helmets included a flared piece at the back to protect the neck—like a firefighter's helmet—as well as a flared piece above the brow to protect the nose and eyes. Cheek pieces were attached to the sides to protect the jaw. A chinstrap secured the helmet onto the soldier's head.

In Ephesians 6:17, Paul referred to this part of our spiritual armor as "the helmet of salvation." But since he is writing to those who have already been saved, why does Paul link the helmet to salvation? What is the relationship between the "helmet of salvation" and the protection of our thoughts?

The moment we place our faith in Christ, we are saved from the guilt of sin—eternal condemnation. But I think Paul has more in mind than the salvation from the *penalty* of sin we immediately receive when we trust in Jesus Christ for our forgiveness. I think he is referring to the fact that we are also saved from the *power* of sin.

You see, every choice we make begins with a thought. As we saw in chapter 1, the mind is command central. It's no surprise, then, that our thoughts are a primary target of Satan's attacks. Because our sin nature longs to yield to the temptations of Satan, we must continually engage our minds with God's Word as we struggle against Satan's enticements and strive to avoid surrendering to sinful habits or addictions.

People all around us excuse sinful behaviors by saying, "You don't have a choice; you must give in." When it comes to venting our anger, refusing to forgive, or indulging in other sins and addictions, the prevailing attitude today is, "It's okay. You're only human." However, the Word of God assures us that salvation is not only for the hereafter but also for the here and now. The same power that raised Jesus from the dead—and will one day resurrect our bodies from the grave—is alive and working in our lives right now, offering us freedom from the power of sin.

How can we put on the helmet of salvation in our everyday lives? We do it by confronting the Enemy's lies with God's truth. We call on God and ask Him for the wisdom to control our thoughts—to "[take] every thought captive to the obedience of Christ" (2 Cor. 10:5).

6. Take Up the Sword of the Spirit

Everything in the inventory of our armory in Ephesians 6 thus far has been defensive. Now Paul introduces us to an offensive weapon—a short, two-edged sword called a *machaira*. In close-quarters combat, the *machaira* was an effective thrusting and slashing weapon.

The Christian's only offensive weapon is "the sword of the Spirit," which Paul said is "the word of God" (Eph. 6:17). The Greek term for "word" in this verse is *rhema*, not *logos*. *Logos* refers to either the written Word of God (Scripture) or the living Word of God (Jesus). *Rhema*, on the other hand, refers to the appropriate Scripture passage that is spoken or applied against a specific temptation. The Holy Spirit impresses specific verses on the hearts and minds of God's people, so that they might apply them at appropriate times to deflect Satan's attacks.

Paul said in 2 Timothy 3:16–17, "All Scripture is inspired by God and profitable for teaching, for reproof, for correction, for training in righteousness; so that the man of God may be adequate, equipped for every good work." The Holy Spirit empowers the use of Scripture in our hearts and lives, making our mouths "like a sharp sword" (Isa. 49:2).

Relying on the Armor of God . . . and the People of God

Perhaps no other person in Scripture embodies the strategies for defeating Satan's attacks outlined by Paul than Paul himself. Paul wrote from personal experience about what it was like to thrive in a world in which we struggle against the Enemy's temptations, a secular agenda, and our own sinful impulses. And perhaps more than any other apostle, Paul suffered for his commitment to Christ.

Writing to the church at Corinth, Paul described some of the hardships he faced:

> Five times I received from the Jews thirty-nine lashes. Three times I was beaten with rods, once I was stoned, three times I was shipwrecked, a night and a day I have spent in the deep. I have been on frequent journeys, in dangers from rivers, dangers from robbers, dangers from my countrymen, dangers from the Gentiles, dangers in the city, dangers in the wilderness, dangers on the sea, dangers among false brethren; I have been in labor and hardship, through many sleepless nights, in hunger and thirst, often without food, in cold and exposure. Apart from such external things, there is the daily pressure on me of concern for all the churches. (2 Cor. 11:24–28)

Paul experienced extreme persecution and suffered for his faith. But through it all, Paul took an inventory of what God had given him. He understood that his spiritual tools included not only the armor of God but also the people of God—his friends.

Paul's letters are filled with the names of people who encouraged and ministered to him, such as Timothy and Titus, Priscilla and Aquila, Philemon and Barnabas, and Mark and Luke. These are just a few of the people who strengthened and reassured Paul during some of his darkest days.[6]

In Romans 12:5, Paul referred to the church as "one body in Christ." Using this metaphor, he explained that Christ is the head, and we are the various members of His body. Because believers in Jesus Christ are all one body—though different members, with different functions—"the members [ought to] have the same care for one another" (1 Cor. 12:25).

The church is a community of believers who are unified in our love and our commitment to Jesus Christ. This is why Paul admonished us to "Rejoice with those who rejoice, and weep with those who weep" (Rom. 12:15). Or, as he wrote elsewhere, "Bear one another's burdens . . . while we have opportunity, let us do good to all people, and especially to those who are of the household of the faith" (Gal. 6:2, 10).

There is strength in numbers. Solomon observed in Ecclesiastes 4:9, "Two are better than one because they have a good return for their labor." He went on to explain, "If one can overpower him who is alone, two can resist him. A cord of three strands is not quickly torn apart" (v. 12). The fact is, we need other Christians.

I'm reminded of the story of a father who gave his young son a bundle of sticks and instructed the boy to break them. The boy lifted the bundle up high and smashed it against his knee, only to bruise his knee. He then took the bundle and set it up against the wall and kicked it, but he had no success breaking the bundle that way either. He tried several other approaches, all unsuccessful in breaking the sticks. When the father returned, he took the bundle of sticks from his son, untied them, and then began to break them very easily, one at a time. What a great picture of the body of Christ! When we are joined together with other Christians, we are strong. But when we are unbundled, untied, and separated from other Christians, we can be easily broken.

For example, two Christians have a disagreement, and those differences cause them to separate. What happens to one or both parties in that relationship? They feel isolated and are more prone to depression, because they are no longer enjoying the friendship that had been so beneficial. Or a believing husband and wife are at odds, and neither will yield their rights to the other. The result is friction and division in the marriage. Each mate feels isolated and emotionally alone, becoming more prone to the temptations of adultery. Or church members don't agree with the direction of the church, so they separate from the rest of the body of Christ. They no longer receive the nourishment needed from that body or the support from other Christians, and they drift into disobedience and sin.

Satan has a three-pronged strategy: divide, isolate, and attack. One thing the Bible makes clear about the church is this: we need one another. Christians need to remain united with one another to resist Satan's temptations and attacks. That's why the writer of the book of Hebrews instructed us to "consider how to stimulate one another to love and good deeds, not forsaking our own assembling together . . . but encouraging one another" (10:24–25).

We have been adopted into God's family, so those who sit next to us in church are not merely friends or acquaintances. If they have made a commitment to Jesus, they are our brothers and sisters. And family members love and care for one another.

Paul concluded his inventory of our spiritual armor by instructing us to "be on the alert with all perseverance and petition for all the saints" (Eph. 6:18). Like a lion that separates the weak and sick from the herd because they are easy to devour, Satan seeks to separate believers from the people of God. But we must never try to stand alone; that is why God gave us the body of Christ.

A Spiritual Inventory

Whether we like it or not, the moment we committed our lives to Christ, Satan put our names on his hit list. And he will hit us with every weapon in his arsenal. He will corrupt the culture. He will try to convince our children that freedom is found in rebellion against God. He will attempt to destroy marriages through pornography or adultery. He will try to persuade those in business that the way to get ahead is to cheat, lie, and steal. And he will do everything within his power to divide churches—to separate the people of God.

When you take inventory of the spiritual tools God has given you, could you honestly say that you are fully equipped to stand firm against Satan's schemes?

- Are you regularly reading, memorizing, and meditating on God's Word (the belt of truth) so that you can confront destructive thoughts with God's truth?

- How obedient are you to God's commands (the breastplate of righteousness)? Are there "chinks" in your life—areas of disobedience—that Satan could use to destroy your faith, your family, and your future?

- How committed are you to God's mission to reach people with the good news of Jesus Christ (the boots of the gospel)? What specific plan do you have to share your faith with those in your circle of influence?

- Do you possess a strong faith, the kind that can deflect satanic attacks (the shield of faith)? What specific promises of God are you relying on right now in spite of the attacks Satan has launched against you?

- Are you acting consistently with the truth that you have been saved not only from the penalty of sin but from the power of sin (the helmet of salvation)? Is there any habit or addiction in your life that you have surrendered to?

- Can you immediately recall specific passages of Scripture to use when you are tempted with lust, greed, anger, doubt, fear, or other temptations (the sword of the Spirit)?

- Are you actively involved in a local church in which you can experience the spiritual strength, accountability, and prayers of other members of the body of Christ (perseverance and petition for all the saints)?

The equipment God has provided for us is more than enough to defeat the Enemy's attacks. Whenever we face challenging situations, we can take inventory of the tools God has supplied us and choose ways to apply them to our lives. And we must courageously put on God's armor and rely on it daily, because spiritual victory only comes to believers who are equipped for the battle.

Develop a Victor,
Not a Victim Mindset

The ship was doomed. Everybody knew it, but there was nothing they could do about it.

For the past year, the *Endurance* had been home to the captain and twenty-seven crew members on a voyage from England to Antarctica. The vessel had sailed twelve thousand miles and then pushed through pack ice for a thousand more, but now it was entombed in the frozen Antarctic—less than one hundred miles from its intended destination. The currents under the icebound sea pushed and pulled against the wooden hull, slowly crushing it. Everyone on board took what supplies they could and abandoned ship, casting their lot to the same ice that held the *Endurance* in its frozen grip.

As they watched the sides of their ship cave in from the pressure and heard the large timbers snap, the men became resigned to what they believed was their inevitable fate: death—either by exposure, starvation, or drowning.

But their leader had a different mindset. "Optimism," he would often say, "is true moral courage."[1] And if there was one thing that was true about Ernest Shackleton, it's that he was an optimist.

Shackleton had set out to be the first man to reach the South Pole, but that honor went to Norwegian explorer Roald Amundsen in 1911. Undeterred, Shackleton set his sights on being the first man to cross Antarctica on foot. But finding supporters to fund his journey proved difficult. It took two years of asking, pleading, and lobbying before Shackleton finally raised enough money to supply his expedition and purchase the Arctic vessel *Polaris*, which he re-christened *Endurance* after his family's motto—*Fortitudine Vincimus*: "By endurance we conquer."[2]

Finding crew members to accompany him was easy. Legend has it that Shackleton placed the following advertisement in the *London Times*:

> Men wanted for hazardous journey to South Pole. Small wages, bitter cold, long months of complete darkness, constant danger. Safe return doubtful. Honor and recognition in case of success.[3]

Shackleton was inundated with more than five thousand applicants.

Fully equipped, and with a crew of twenty-seven adventurers, the *Endurance* sailed from Plymouth, England, in August 1914. By January of the following year, the ship was icebound.

The crew members built a galley and storehouse out of the ship's timbers and braved six months on the ice, surviving on salvaged rations until the ice thinned enough for them to try to reach Elephant Island in the lifeboats they had scavenged from the *Endurance*. But when the frostbitten men finally reached Elephant Island, it turned out to be a frozen wasteland, without any sustainable food stores.

To rescue his men from exposure and starvation—and certain death—Shackleton, with a small crew, boarded a lifeboat and sailed 870 miles to South Georgia Island, where there was a whaling station with supplies. The journey took seventeen days, and they landed under hurricane conditions. However, the whaling station was on the other side of the island, so Shackleton and his crew had to traverse thirty-two miles over glacier-covered peaks. It took another four months before Shackleton finally reached his stranded men on Elephant Island with the supplies they needed and carried them back to England.

Although Shackleton did not succeed in his mission to cross Antarctica on foot, he did save the lives of all twenty-seven crew members. Years later, one of the men called him "the greatest leader that ever came on God's earth, bar none." He wrote, "When you are in a hopeless situation, when there seems no way out, get down on your knees and pray for Shackleton."[4]

Our Attitude Is Essential to Survival

Ernest Shackleton realized an important truth: our attitude is essential to our survival. After an earlier but equally ill-fated Antarctic expedition, Shackleton wrote, "Difficulties are just things to overcome."[5] Shackleton and his crew faced challenges that were as crushing as the ice that destroyed their ship: subzero temperatures, scant provisions, the impossibility of resupply, no radio to signal for help, and tempest-tossed oceans that stretched for hundreds of miles. No matter the circumstances, Shackleton determined to overcome—and to do it with cheer and courage.

Shackleton had something that everybody who survives difficult times must possess: a fighting spirit—an optimistic stubbornness that, come what may, refuses to give in to helplessness and hopelessness. He had stripped *can't*, *never*, and *surrender* from his vocabulary. There is no record of him ever seeing himself as a victim. Shackleton understood that difficulties arise because of the foolish choices we make, the foolish choices others make, or the simple fact that we live in an imperfect world. Shackleton had carefully planned his expedition and had provided sufficient provisions to complete the journey. But he also knew that Antarctic expeditions were inherently dangerous, and things were bound to go awry. The key to survival was knowing how to respond when things didn't go as planned.

The same is true in our lives. When difficulties come—whether from our own failures, the failures of others, or the fact that the world is broken—we should never see ourselves as victims. Rather, we are to remember that "God is for us" (Rom. 8:31). No matter what circumstances we face, we can choose to have the mindset of victors, not victims.

Our Attitude Determines Our Character

Someone once said that musicians can't talk themselves into a great performance, but they can talk themselves out of one! I have experienced the truth of those words. Though I'm not a classically trained musician, I have played the accordion since I was five. During my younger years, I earned quite a bit of money playing my accordion for weddings, bar mitzvahs, and various other events. Occasionally, I would play wrong notes—especially when I was learning a new piece—but I learned not to dwell on those mistakes. The problem with obsessing over a wrong note is that it has a cascading effect: one wrong note leads to another wrong note, which in turn leads to another wrong note . . . until the piece becomes a disaster. Instead, I would heed the advice of my accordion teacher, Al Trick, who used to tell me, "Just keep smiling while you're playing, and the audience won't know the difference!"

When I think about my teacher's advice, it reminds me of the importance of our attitude. What is attitude? Here is a good definition: *attitude is our mental and emotional response to the circumstances of life.* We cannot change many of the circumstances we face in life, but we can choose whether to allow those circumstances to strengthen us or destroy us.

Here's how Chuck Swindoll put it: "The longer I live the more convinced I become that life is 10 percent what happens to us and 90 percent how we respond to it."[6] Our attitude determines more than our actions; it also determines our character. Some people are confirmed pessimists. They decide to have a negative response to every circumstance. Yet other people can look at the same circumstances and choose a positive outlook.

Throughout the Bible, we are encouraged to choose the attitude of overcomers and victors. Let's look at what the apostle John said about the importance of our attitude.

We Are Overcomers

While he was exiled on the island of Patmos, John wrote a letter to the churches in Asia Minor. The churches at that time were being bombarded with a false teaching called Gnosticism, a belief that spiritual things were good and holy while physical things were corrupt and evil. Many Gnostics taught that since only the spiritual aspect of people was holy, it didn't matter what believers did with their physical bodies.

John's answer to the Gnostics was swift and strong: if you claim to love God, then you will obey God's commands—including the ones regarding your body—because you have overcome the world. In 1 John 5:3–5, he wrote, "In fact, this is love for God: to keep his commands. And his commands are not burdensome, for everyone born of God overcomes the world. This is the victory that has overcome the world, even our faith. Who is it that has overcome the world? Only the one who believes that Jesus is the Son of God?" (NIV).

The Greek word translated "overcomes" in this passage means "to come off victorious." John was not saying that there is a class of special Christians called "overcomers" who are victorious, in contrast to those who are defeated. Rather, John uses the word as a synonym for all true believers. Through our faith in Jesus Christ, we are all victors.

It is important to understand that faith is more than simply agreeing with what God says is true. As we saw in an earlier chapter, faith is believing what God says and *acting accordingly*, regardless of the consequences. Put practically, our faith is the way we can thrive in a world that brings despair, depression, and defeat.

In verse 3, John said that the Lord's commands "are not burdensome" for those who truly love God. When we have faith that our heavenly Father wants what is best for us, we will gladly submit to His commands.

This reminds me of the all-night search for an eight-year-old boy named Dominic, who was on a ski trip with his father. Dominic had ridden a new lift and apparently veered off the marked ski trail without realizing it. For hours, a ninety-person search team scoured the mountain but found no trace of him. Finally, when two helicopters joined the search at dawn, they spotted ski tracks. A ground team hurriedly followed the tracks, which led to a tree—where they found the boy in good shape.

In an interview, the search-and-rescue coordinator explained why the boy had survived so well despite spending a night in the freezing elements. Dominic's father had enough forethought to tell the boy what to do if he became lost, and his son had enough trust to do exactly what his father said.

Dominic had protected himself from possible frostbite and hypothermia by snuggling up to a tree and covering himself with branches. As a young child, he likely would not have thought of doing this on his own. He was simply obeying the instructions from his wise and loving father, trusting that his father knew what was best for him.[7]

John said that those who belong to God will trust our heavenly Father and follow His instructions: "By this we know that we love the children of God, when we love God and observe His commandments" (1 John 5:2). As God's children, we share in His victory—a victory that comes by our faith in Jesus, who has already "overcome the world" (John 16:33).

God can use even the most difficult situations in our lives for our good and His glory. That's the promise of Romans 8:28: "God causes all things to work together for good to those who love God, to those who are called according to His purpose." And what is the highest good God could imagine coming out of our trials? Paul provided the answer in verse 29: that we might "become conformed to the image of His Son." God's purpose is to use every circumstance we face to mold our character to become more like Jesus Christ.

We may not always be able to change our circumstances, but we can change our attitudes. And changed attitudes result in changed lives.

Joseph: "God Meant It for Good"

Perhaps no person in all of Scripture, next to the Lord Jesus Christ, had a more victorious attitude in the face of difficult circumstances than the Old Testament patriarch Joseph. Though the Bible never mentions Joseph seeing himself as a victim, Genesis 37–50 makes it clear that he knew the pain of victimization. Between the ages of seventeen and thirty, Joseph courageously endured what must have seemed like a never-ending series of injustices. For thirteen long years, he spent his life either in a pit, as another man's property, or in a prison.

The difficult situation you may be facing right now is no doubt different from Joseph's, but the injustices that led to these experiences are common to everybody. If you live long enough, you will understand the sting of unfair treatment and will suffer unforeseen consequences, as Joseph did. Let's look at the three sources of Joseph's problems that are common to all of us.

Unloving Actions from Family

Joseph's brothers were jealous of him because he was the favorite son—a status that Genesis 37:3 makes clear: "Israel [Jacob] loved Joseph more than all his sons, because he was the son of his old age." As we see in this story, one of the great dangers of showing favoritism toward a child is not only what it does to your other children but what it does to the favored child.

Jacob gave Joseph a "varicolored tunic" (v. 3). This coat was more than just a gift from a loving father. The colorful tunic, which was similar to ones worn by the nobility of the day, was a symbol of Joseph's authority over his brothers, exempting him from the hard, dirty work of shepherding. Every time Joseph's brothers saw him strutting around in that coat, anger and resentment welled up in them. This is a lesson for us parents: be careful not to show favoritism among your children.

Morning after morning, the brothers dressed to tend flocks under the hot desert sun while Joseph lounged around the tent in his beautiful tunic. Then one day, while the brothers were out working in the field, Jacob sent Joseph to check on them. When they looked off in the distance and saw their brother in his special coat, Joseph's brothers vowed to get their revenge. They devised a plan to kill him, throw his body into a pit, and cover their crime with a lie. However, one of the brothers, Reuben, persuaded them not to kill Joseph and suggested they just leave him in the pit.

When Joseph reached his brothers, they pounced on him, pulled off his tunic, and threw him into an empty water cistern. Then they decided to let him suffer in the pit while they ate lunch. How could they do that with a clear conscience? It's easy to blame the brothers, but the truth is, we all have a tremendous ability to rationalize sin. We point to people who are worse than we are and say, "We're pretty good compared to them." I am sure the brothers said, "Hey, we were going to kill him, but we only put him in a pit." This is a reminder that we have our own standards of behavior, but God has a standard of behavior that is far different from ours.

While the brothers were eating, they saw a caravan of Ishmaelite traders passing by. Judah, sensing an opportunity not only to get rid of their bothersome little brother but also to make a few shekels in the process, convinced the others to sell Joseph as a slave. They agreed and were paid twenty pieces of silver for him.

They decided to tell their father that a wild animal had killed Joseph. To cover up the lie, they shredded Joseph's coat and dipped it in goat's blood. When Jacob saw the blood-stained coat and heard his sons' gruesome report, he "mourned for his son many days" (v. 34).

Imagine yourself in Joseph's place for just a moment. You had a great life as the favored son in a wealthy family. Then, all of a sudden, your brothers betrayed you, threw you in a pit, and left you for dead before they sold you to slave traders who took you to a foreign country, where you ended up surrounded by strangers speaking an unfamiliar language. Talk about a bad day! If this had happened to you, wouldn't you be tempted to have a victim mindset? Remember, Joseph didn't know how his story was going to turn out. As far as he knew, his life was over. But the Bible never records Joseph throwing a pity party for himself.

When God sends tests into our lives, they usually involve a change we could never have anticipated. You may be experiencing that right now. Things were going along just fine when, out of nowhere, you were ambushed by an unexpected problem. Perhaps it was a pink slip from your employer or a huge loss in your retirement savings. Perhaps a sudden illness struck you or a loved one. Maybe it's an unexpected divorce. Whatever the reason, you are in a place you never anticipated, and you can empathize with Joseph's situation.

Notice, though, what Genesis 39:2 says about God: "The LORD was with Joseph." Even in the darkest of circumstances, God had a plan for Joseph. And when you and I find ourselves in a pit of trials, instead of seeing ourselves as victims, we can take courage in knowing that He has a plan for us as well.

Unfair Accusations from Others

In Egypt, Joseph was sold as a slave to Potiphar, the captain of Pharaoh's bodyguard. Joseph quickly began distinguishing himself as a wise and diligent servant in Potiphar's house. In fact, Joseph was so trustworthy that Potiphar placed him over his entire household.

The only thing off-limits to Joseph was Potiphar's wife. But Mrs. Potiphar didn't think Joseph was off-limits to *her*. This Hebrew teenager was "handsome in form and appearance" (v. 6). One day, catching him alone, she said to Joseph, "Lie with me" (v. 7). Joseph's refusal was as straightforward as her invitation: "How then could I do this great evil and sin against God?" (v. 9).

But a brazen woman is not easily dissuaded! Mrs. Potiphar enticed Joseph day after day. And day after day, Joseph refused. Seeing that her silky-smooth words had no effect, she decided to change tactics: she would throw herself at him. One day, when they were alone in the house, she grabbed Joseph by his robe. He ran so quickly in the opposite direction that she was left with nothing but his empty robe and her bruised ego.

No sooner had Joseph cleared the door than he heard her scream . . . and so did the other servants. They came running to see what was wrong. Mrs. Potiphar claimed that Joseph had tried to rape her, and she had the "evidence" to prove it—his garment. When her husband came home, Mrs. Potiphar repeated her story to him, and Potiphar threw Joseph into prison.

Joseph's experience helps us understand an important biblical truth: obedience to God doesn't always result in a happy ending—at least immediately. Now, if you disobey God and suffer negative consequences, then that is not suffering; that is justice. You don't get any brownie points for that. There are a lot of Christians who were lazy at their job and got fired, or they were unfaithful to their mate and ended up divorced, or they didn't pay their taxes and wound up in prison. "I'm suffering for Jesus," they say. No, they are suffering for their bad choices.

Suffering for Christ is when you experience negative consequences for doing what is right. You obey God, yet you still suffer for it. That's how Christ suffered. When Jesus died on the cross, He wasn't suffering for doing what was wrong, as the other criminals were; He was suffering for doing what was right. And that is the kind of suffering Jesus plans for you and me.

God was preparing Joseph for the role He had planned for him, and that meant going through a time of suffering for doing what was right. You may be suffering for doing right and wondering, "What's going on, God? Why aren't You rewarding me for obeying You?" You may feel like you have good reason to give in to a victim mindset. But remember, just as the final chapter was not yet written in Joseph's story in Genesis 39, the final chapter in your life has not yet been revealed. And just as God was with Joseph, God is with you.

Unfair Neglect by Friends

Joseph distinguished himself in prison and proved to be a model inmate. The warden even gave Joseph the keys to the place.

While he was performing his work in the prison, two new prisoners were added—Pharaoh's chief cupbearer and chief baker. One night, both the baker and cupbearer had disturbing dreams. Joseph said God could interpret their dreams and offered to help them understand their meanings. The cupbearer said he dreamed about squeezing grapes into a cup and placing the cup in Pharaoh's hand. Joseph predicted that the cupbearer would be restored to his position in three days. The baker said he dreamed of baskets of bread, some of which were being eaten by birds. Joseph said that the baker would be killed in three days.

Just as Joseph predicted, within three days, the baker was executed, and the cupbearer was released to return to the palace. Before the cupbearer left the prison, Joseph asked him to put in a good word with Pharaoh, since he had been unlawfully sold as a slave and was now unlawfully imprisoned. But the cupbearer forgot Joseph. So Joseph remained in prison for "two full years," forgotten by friends and feeling forsaken by God (41:1).

Let's be honest: at this point in Joseph's story, most of us would probably give Joseph a pass if he had developed a "woe is me" mindset and given in to self-pity. But even in these challenging circumstances, Joseph chose to trust God.

When suffering comes in our lives, we tend to think, *This is unfair! God, why are You allowing this?* Maybe you are in that spot right now. Maybe you are in a crisis. You cry out to God, but there is no answer. As the days turn into weeks and the weeks turn into months, you wonder, *Where is God when I need Him most?*

Like Joseph, you can't imagine the plans God has for you, but you can know for sure that God has not forgotten you. Even circumstances that are unexpected and seem unfair and unbearable are part of God's plan for you. Romans 8:28–29 says God's purpose is to shape you into the image of His Son. That's what God was doing in Joseph's life, and that's what God is doing in your life as well.

From Prison to the Palace

After what must have been the two longest years in Joseph's life, Pharaoh had two disturbing dreams. None of his wise men or magicians could tell him what the dreams meant. Then the cupbearer remembered Joseph and recommended his dream interpretation skill to Pharaoh.

Joseph was summoned into the throne room and coura- geously stood before the most powerful man in the world. Pharaoh said to him, "I have heard it said . . . that when you hear a dream you can interpret it" (41:15). Joseph re- spectfully corrected Pharaoh: "It is not in me; God will give Pharaoh a favorable answer" (v. 16). Then Pharaoh told Jo- seph his dreams.

Joseph, in turn, through the wisdom of God, told Pharaoh the interpretation of his dreams: seven years of abundant harvest in the land would be followed by seven years of fam- ine. For the kingdom to survive those lean years, Joseph advised the king to find a wise person to be in charge of storing the excess grain during the years of abundance and distributing it to the people during the years of scarcity.

Pharaoh didn't have to look far to find such a person; he was standing right in front of him. And with the snap of Pharaoh's fingers, Joseph was made the prime minister of Egypt. Twenty-four hours earlier he had been in prison: forgotten and forsaken, he thought, forever. The next day, he was appointed to be the second-in-command to Pharaoh.

Why is this story in the Bible? Certainly, it reminds us that God is in control of everyone and everything. But this story also assures us that we can maintain the mindset of a victor no matter what circumstances we face in life, because God exalts His servants in His way and in His time.

How to Think Like a Victor

Chances are you've never been thrown into a pit or sold into slavery. And you probably haven't spent multiple years in prison for a crime you didn't commit. But you have felt the sting of unloving words and actions from those who should love you. You may have had your heart broken by a sibling or parent. You know the frustration that family squabbles can bring, as well as the disappointments and embarrassments of generational family sins.

And no doubt your name has come up as a matter of gossip or ridicule at some point in your life. Others have talked about you behind your back. They've falsely accused you of wrongdoing or having ulterior motives. And with each betrayal, you've felt humiliated and shamed.

You also likely know the disillusionment of being forgotten and abandoned by friends. The people you helped offered no gratitude, and their helping hand wasn't there when you needed it. You and I are often stuck, like the crew members of the *Endurance*, in situations we cannot do anything about. Life in this world is hard and unfair. We can't change that. The only thing we can change is our attitude.

How will you respond when people do and say hateful things, when others "insult you and persecute you, and falsely say all kinds of evil against you" (Matt. 5:11)? Will you rage and shake your fist, or will you hang your head in resignation? Will you crawl into bed, refusing to get out? Will you see yourself as a victim and act like one? Or, like Ernest Shackleton and the Old Testament Joseph, are you made of sterner stuff?

I'm convinced that, more than ever, we live at a time when victimhood is celebrated. There's even a name for people who seemingly cannot cope with the difficulties of life: "snowflakes." These people are self-obsessed, easily offended, and retreat to so-called safe spaces when they are unable to cope with opposing viewpoints. Actions like these perpetuate the general notion in our culture that we are all victims—victims of our parents' shortcomings, victims of our society's ills, and victims of poor education, hypocritical churches, or government incompetence and corruption.

Nonsense! I don't need to tell you that we live in a broken world. Bad things happen, whether on a global, national, or personal scale. Nowhere in the Bible has God promised to heal every physical infirmity, restore every broken relationship, or replenish every depleted bank account. But as I explained earlier, as Christians, you and I are not to fall into despair or live as victims. Real faith means allowing God the freedom to do what is best in your life. And God grants victory to those who exercise faith.

Some of you reading this book may not be followers of Jesus. For you, it's impossible to live as a victor as John described and as Joseph demonstrated. I encourage you, before you read another sentence, to trust your eternal destiny into the hands of Jesus Christ. He died so your sins might be forgiven, and He rose from the dead so you might have heavenly life. There are no magic words to say or secret handshakes to learn. The apostle Paul said it's easy: "If you confess with your mouth Jesus as Lord, and believe in your heart that God raised Him from the dead, you will be saved" (Rom. 10:9). In Acts 16:31, Paul stated it in even simpler terms: "Believe in the Lord Jesus, and you will be saved."

When we come to Christ, He gives us the greatest gift we will ever receive: the presence and power of the Holy Spirit. And because we have the Spirit of God in our lives, we no longer need to be victims of sin—whether our own or someone else's.

But that is just the first step in thinking like a victor. We also need to develop mental toughness. We could call this tenacity. The word comes from the Latin *tenacitas*, meaning "holding fast." When I think of tenacity, I picture former British prime minister Winston Churchill. A man who overcame great difficulties and personal suffering, Churchill became known as the "British Bulldog." His mental toughness, courage, and determination emboldened the Allies to defeat the powerful Nazi forces in World War II. "Do you know why the English Bulldog has a jutting chin and sloping face?" he reportedly asked while addressing a Nazi envoy in 1940. "It is so he can breathe without letting go."[8]

Three Responses of a Victor

Victors don't feel sorry for themselves, and they don't quit. They persist. Persistence is the courage to continue pursuing your goal in spite of unexpected setbacks, undeserved criticism, and unrelenting hard work.

How does this apply to you and me as we seek to survive the challenges that come into our lives? Based on what we've learned in this chapter, let's look at three ways we can choose the mindset of a victor, not a victim.

 Victors Keep God's Commandments

First, victors keep God's commandments. Remember, faith isn't merely agreeing with what God says is true; faith is acting on what God says to do. In other words, when we are facing troublesome circumstances, we choose to get hold of God's Word and allow it to get hold of us.

Joseph did this when he was tempted time and again by Potiphar's wife. When she tried to seduce him, he said, "How then could I do this great evil and sin against God?" (Gen. 39:9). Then he ran as far and as fast as he could from the source of his temptation

The apostle Paul had the same advice for his protégé, Timothy. When we are in a potentially dangerous situation, we don't analyze the temptation or try to disarm the temptation but run from the temptation. As Paul put it in 2 Timothy 2:22: "Flee from youthful lusts and pursue righteousness."

Many years later, when Joseph had an opportunity to seek vengeance against his brothers for their mistreatment, he chose to forgive them. Why? Joseph believed in a God who was more powerful than his brothers—a God who was able to take the hurts inflicted by others and use them for Joseph's good and for God's glory. Only when you have faith that God is bigger than your offenders can you obey God's command to "be kind to one another, tender-hearted, forgiving each other, just as God in Christ also has forgiven you" (Eph. 4:32).

Victors Glorify God in Their Lives

Second, victors glorify God in their lives. Put simply, to glorify God means to shine the spotlight on God. The only reason God left us here on earth after saving us is so that we might cause others to see Him and be attracted to Him. When we fully grasp that our purpose in life is to glorify God, then we start viewing our challenges, hardships, and sufferings as opportunities to shine the spotlight on God's power and grace working through our lives.

In describing Joseph's ordeal as a slave and a prisoner, the book of Genesis repeats this phrase: "The LORD was with Joseph" (39:2, 3, 21, 23). Why was God with Joseph? Because Joseph chose to glorify God in all he did and said, whether he was refusing Mrs. Potiphar's advances, working diligently as a slave in Potiphar's house, serving as a prisoner in jail, or leading as prime minister of Egypt.

Victors choose to have an attitude that gives glory to God, no matter the situation. They understand and apply Paul's command in 1 Corinthians 10:31: "Whether, then, you eat or drink or whatever you do, do all to the glory of God."

Victors Trust in God's Purposes

Finally, victors trust in God's purposes. As we have seen, the fundamental reason God allows you and me to go through difficulties is to make us more like Christ.

I think about the sculptor who was able to chisel a life-like image of a lion out of a slab of marble. Someone asked him how he was able to sculpt such a realistic figure. "It's easy," the sculptor replied. "I just chisel away everything that doesn't look like a lion." Similarly, God is in the process of sculpting us into a perfect reproduction of His Son, whom He loves dearly. How does God make us look like Jesus? By using the heavy blows of His hammer and chisel to remove any attitudes, actions, or affections in our lives that are not like Jesus's.

God may bring other good out of our hardships as well. This was certainly true of Joseph, who was able to look back on the painful events of his life and see how God used his brothers' wrong motivations and wrong actions to place Joseph in Egypt as Pharaoh's right-hand man. Through Joseph's wise advice about storing grain, Egypt and the early Jewish nation through Jacob and his sons were saved. Joseph said, "As for you, you meant evil against me, but God meant it for good in order to bring about this present result, to preserve many people alive" (Gen. 50:20). That's a victor's mentality if there ever was one.

Our attitude, especially when facing hardships in life, can make the difference between simply surviving and thriving. If you and I are going to thrive in this hostile world, we must resist the temptation to see ourselves as victims of other people's actions or of circumstances that are beyond our control. Instead, we need to choose to develop and maintain a victor's mindset that keeps our focus on God by obeying His commands and trusting in His purpose in everything He allows into our lives.

Trust Your Training

He had no ambition to become famous—to be interviewed by journalists around the world, receive honors and medals, appear on the cover of magazines, or have a movie made about him. After more than forty years as a pilot, his only ambition was retirement. And he was about one year away from that goal when the unimaginable happened—a complete loss of power while piloting a jetliner over Manhattan. In about the same time it takes me to comb my hair, floss, and brush my teeth, the pilot of US Airways 1549 had to decide whether he could keep the plane in the air long enough to turn back to the airport or risk the lives of all 155 people on board with a hazardous water landing.

Departing on the afternoon of January 15, 2009, from New York's LaGuardia Airport bound for Charlotte, North Carolina, Flight 1549 flew into a flock of Canadian geese just two minutes after takeoff. Some of the geese were sucked into the plane's engines. Almost immediately, the aircraft began to vibrate, and the engines shut down.

Twenty-one seconds later, Captain Chesley "Sully" Sullenberger sent out a distress signal: "Mayday! Mayday! Mayday!" He notified the tower at LaGuardia that they had sustained multiple bird strikes and that his plane had become a "dead stick." Descending at a rapid speed—like dropping two floors per second in an elevator—Captain Sullenberger considered gliding the airplane back to LaGuardia, but he would have to fly a dead plane over densely populated areas in Manhattan, avoiding skyscrapers between his location and the airport. LaGuardia was out of the question. Nor could he make it to Teterboro Airport in New Jersey. Sullenberger radioed the tower: he was going to ditch in the Hudson River—it was straight enough, long enough, wide enough, and smooth enough. And besides, it was right below him.

According to aviation experts, successful water landings are tricky maneuvers. Wings have to be perfectly level. If not, you could clip the water, shearing off the wing, cartwheeling the aircraft, and sending the fuselage to the bottom. The angle of entry must be exactly right. If too steep, you can separate the tail section. If too flat, you could break the aircraft in half or plow the nose into what might as well be a concrete wall. You have to "walk" the plane into the water, heel-to-toe, with the tail section touching first and then lowering the nose as the aircraft slows down.

The only control Captain Sullenberger had left in the aircraft was pitch—the ability to raise or lower the nose of the plane. To slow their speed and maintain a proper glide angle, Sullenberger pitched the nose up. About ninety seconds before hitting the water, he pulled the nose fully aft—back—and addressed the passengers: "This is the captain. Brace for impact."

Passengers described what felt like a gradual, controlled descent, as if the river were a tarmac. And though the airplane made a tremendous splash, it remained intact and afloat. Once the aircraft became stable, Sullenberger and his crew began emergency evacuation procedures—instructing passengers about how to locate and wear life vests, deploy emergency rafts, and open wing exits. Fortunately, the plane had landed between two ferry terminals. Within minutes, ferryboats were plucking passengers off the wings and out of the rafts, saving all 155 people on board.

Sullenberger—who learned to fly at the age of sixteen, graduated from the Air Force Academy, and flew fighter jets before turning to commercial aviation—has been asked many times what he was thinking during the three-and-a-half minutes that elapsed between his engines cutting out and landing in the Hudson River. His standard answer is that he wasn't so much thinking as acting, going through the proper procedures to solve the problems that immediately confronted him. He said, "My training kicked in."[1]

Trust Your Training

Know what do it[1]

When thrown into survival situations, police officers, firefighters, and military personnel often encourage one another with three simple words: "Trust your training." Athletes also build muscle memory through disciplined training. When the pressure is on to perform, first responders and athletes don't necessarily think about what to do next; they react according to how they have trained their minds and muscles to respond in those situations.

This is the reason people say, "Practice makes perfect." Practicing correctly trains our minds and muscles to respond correctly when situations call for it. Practice is power because it provides a level of control during stressful situations. For Captain Sullenberger, years of piloting aircraft and successfully solving in-flight problems gave him a sense of control when his plane lost power over Manhattan. In fact, Sullenberger's courageous actions are a good illustration of the survival tips we have discussed so far in this book.

- Survival Tip #1—he didn't panic. He remained cool and controlled even though he only had about 210 seconds to land his plane safely.
- Survival Tip #2—he quickly apprised his situation: bird strike, loss of power, too far to make airports, losing altitude quickly, and the Hudson River as his best option to save passengers and crew.
- Survival Tip #3—he took inventory of what he had available: pitch control, a trained and competent copilot, a trained and competent flight crew, a well-built and safety-equipped aircraft, and decades of flying experience.
- Survival Tip #4—he believed he could successfully complete the water landing and rescue all on board. "I was flying the airplane and I was flying it well," he told *The Guardian*. And when the plane came to rest in the Hudson, he turned to his copilot, Jeffrey Skiles, and said, "It wasn't as bad as we thought."[2]

But it was Sullenberger's reliance on his training that ultimately saved the passengers and crew of Flight 1549. When a sudden crisis hit, Captain Sullenberger trusted his training. You and I must do the same if we hope to survive the unavoidable crises that appear out of nowhere and assault our lives like the flock of geese that struck US Airways 1549.

Whether we survive those assaults affects not only us but also those who are traveling with us. Just as Captain Sullenberger had people who were depending on him to safely land the plane on which they were traveling, you and I have people who are depending on us not to "crash" our lives, including our family, friends, church members, and fellow Christ-followers. Simply put, if we go down, we will likely take them down with us.

Our only hope to survive spiritually is to be sure we are adequately trained for the crisis before it hits and then trust our training when it hits.

Training in God's Word

We are trained spiritually by reading and studying God's Word—our "flight manual," if you will—and then committing His Word to memory. Why is that so important? Just today as I was writing this chapter, I read the account of another airplane mishap, but it did not have the same happy ending as Flight 1549. In October 2018 the pilots of Lion Air flight JT610 experienced an unexpected problem just after takeoff from Jakarta. The jet's automated system kept pointing the nose of the plane downward. The pilots frantically searched the flight manual trying to find the solution to the problem, but time ran out and the 737 jet crashed, killing all 189 people on board.[3]

Just as airline pilots can't afford to spend precious moments searching through an exhaustive flight manual for a chapter on "What to Do When Geese Strike," Christians rarely have time to fumble through God's Word searching for answers ("I know it's in here somewhere!"). And there is no better way to train yourself for spiritual emergencies than by memorizing key portions of God's Word.

Now, I realize this doesn't sound like fun. Neither do eating vegetables and exercising. But if Christians are to survive during these difficult days, we need to have more in our spiritual diet than Häagen-Dazs ice cream (my favorite treat!).

This reminds me of a story a ministry colleague once told me. When he served as a youth pastor, he often took teenagers on mission trips to rural parts of the United States. Every morning, students were required to have personal devotions of Scripture reading and prayer. On one such trip, he walked through the sanctuary of the church where the boys were having their devotions. He came upon one young man lying facedown on a pew, his nose buried in his open Bible. My friend gently shook the young man's shoulder. With a jerk of his head, the young man blurted out, "I'm having my quiet time!" No doubt he was. But the drool on his Bible gave my friend serious doubts about what kind of "quiet time" this young man was having![4] If we are honest, all of us at times have viewed Bible reading as a sure cure for insomnia.

The truth is, memorizing is hard work. For some of us, it conjures up unpleasant images of school—of memorizing parts of speech, multiplication tables, or lines from Shakespeare. However, if we are to survive the cultural and personal challenges facing us today, then we need to rely on more than our wits; we need to rely on the wisdom of God.

And the best way to have immediate access to the wisdom of God, anytime we need it, is by committing God's Word to memory.

Memory is a fascinating function of our brains. Despite the astounding advances we have made in technology, no invention has ever produced anything close to the capability of the human brain. Every morning when you wake up, you remember how to turn on the lights, you remember where the bathroom is, and you remember how the shower works. You go through all the steps of getting ready without really thinking about them, because that information has been tucked away in your memory.[5]

Or consider the process of driving a car. Have you ever ridden in a vehicle with a newly permitted driver? I remember the interesting, and sometimes terrifying, adventure of teaching my teenage daughters to drive. I had to explain everything to them: "This is the steering wheel," "This is the brake," "This is the gas pedal." Every time I sat in the passenger seat to supervise their driving, I would grip the door handle for dear life and say a prayer as they navigated through traffic. They had to think carefully through every single step.

But now, after decades of driving, my daughters easily use turn signals, switch lanes, and stop at red lights, no matter what traffic situation they encounter. A few weeks ago, when I was running errands with my older daughter, I relaxed in the passenger seat, scrolling through my phone and chatting with her as she drove through complex downtown traffic. What made the difference? She has repeated the process of driving so often that she has memorized the steps, and driving has become second nature to her.

Like getting ready for work or driving a car, everything we do relies on information we have stored in our memory. If you and I commit to memorizing the truths of the Bible the way my daughters memorized the details of driving, then we will be able to live out God's Word, as if by second nature, as we navigate through life. Whenever we encounter difficult or tempting times, we can trust our Scripture training.

Let's take a look at three reasons we should go through the training of memorizing Scripture. Each one comes from Psalm 119—a psalm dedicated to the Word of God.

Memorized Scripture Provides Wise Counsel throughout Life

We all wish that life were fair and easy. But it's not, and we know it. That's why we need to hide God's Word in our hearts. Psalm 119:105 says, "Your word is a lamp to my feet and a light to my path." Have you ever been out in the woods on a cloudy night, trying to find your way? It's difficult to see when there is no illumination from above. But hopefully you have a flashlight that governs your steps. That flashlight isn't powerful enough to illuminate the next few miles. But it does give you enough light to take the next step and the next step and the next step.

That's what the psalmist said God's Word is like. God's Word, His communication to us, does not illuminate the rest of our lives. It does not tell us God's entire plan for us. But it gives us just the light we need to take the next step. And it's not our ability to walk on a sunny path that proves our trust in God; it's our ability to walk on a darkened path with just enough light to place one foot in front of the other.

All of us would like to know what the future holds, whether good or bad. But the truth is, none of us knows what even the next few hours will bring. Even before you finish reading this paragraph, you might receive a phone call with devastating news. Or when you open your eyes in the morning, you might not see the familiar surroundings of your bedroom but the spectacular beauty of heaven. Because we don't know what will happen in life, it is essential for us to have a working knowledge of God's Word to guide us and provide wise counsel when we need it.

In the first century, believers routinely memorized various passages from the Old Testament as well as the message of the gospel they had heard from the apostles. Since they had limited access to written Scripture, early Christians had to rely on Scripture memory in order to learn and apply God's Word. Their knowledge of Scripture, which they not only memorized but also recited to one another, helped them through times of difficulties, distress, and even intense persecution.

Today, we think that since we have quick access to the Bible in print or on our smartphones, we don't need to memorize it. But when we neglect our mental muscles, our minds become like erasable whiteboards. We can retain facts for a short period of time, but because we don't commit anything to long-term memory, we soon replace those facts with new information—a process of learning and forgetting that we repeat over and over.[6]

If we are to thrive in these challenging times, it is essential that we exercise our mental muscles to store up the Word of

God for long-term use. The Word of God, especially recalled at a moment's notice, can guide us through uncertain and trying times.

Memorized Scripture Is a Faithful Friend during Difficult Days

Whenever I have gone through challenging times and felt as if a friend was nowhere in sight, I have been comforted by the words of Psalm 119:92–93: "If Your law had not been my delight, then I would have perished in my affliction. I will never forget Your precepts, for by them You have revived me." It's not positive self-talk or the encouragement of others that raises us beyond the harsh realities of life; it's listening to God as we recall His Word to mind.

Why do we turn to the Bible during times of discouragement, confusion, and heartache? Because God, who promised, "I will never desert you, nor will I ever forsake you" (Heb. 13:5), speaks healing and hope through the words in His Book. And when we put some of those words into our hearts, we will never be alone.

Darlene Deibler Rose was a Christian missionary who was captured by the Japanese in World War II and spent four years in a prison camp where she was frequently interrogated and beaten. Although the guards took her Bible, they could not take the verses she had tucked away in her memory.

She later wrote about how those memorized Scriptures gave her courage and comfort when she was placed in solitary confinement.

As a child and young person, I had had a driving compulsion to memorize the written Word. In the cell I was grateful now for those days in Vacation Bible School, when I had memorized many single verses, complete chapters, and Psalms, as well as whole books of the Bible. In the years that followed, I reviewed the Scriptures often. The Lord fed me with the Living Bread that had been stored against the day when fresh supply was cut off by the loss of my Bible. He brought daily comfort and encouragement—yes, and joy to my heart through the knowledge of the Word.[7]

No matter what situation you are facing—whether in the culture, your community, or even in your own home—there is no more faithful friend than the Word of God in your heart.

Memorized Scripture Serves as a Sure Defense against Temptation

In Psalm 119:11, David wrote, "Your word I have treasured in my heart, that I may not sin against You." Being able to trust your training by recalling memorized verses during times of temptation can save you from many troubles.

We can stay strong in survival situations by confronting wrong thoughts with God's Word. The reason we memorize Scripture is not to accumulate knowledge about the Bible so that we can go around impressing one another. No. Mere knowledge of Scripture is not enough to transform us. After all, the apostle James told us, "the demons also believe, and shudder" (James 2:19). The reason we put God's Word into our minds is so that when wrong thoughts come, we can confront them with the truth of God's Word.

The fact is, you can't control a lot of the thoughts that come into your mind. Of course, you can lessen wrong thoughts by avoiding negative people and negative input. But even if you were secluded from every smartphone, television, website, billboard, and magazine, you would still deal with wrong thoughts.

Protestant Reformer Martin Luther once wrote about a young man who was struggling with lustful thoughts and other temptations, so he sought the advice of a hermit. The old man told him, "You can't stop the birds from flying over your head, but only let them fly. Don't let them nest in your hair."[8] In other words, you can't control the thoughts that come into your mind, but you can control what you do with those thoughts. You can allow sinful thoughts to linger in your mind. You can elaborate on them and embellish them until they metastasize into a full-blown case of sin that you act on. Or you can confront those wrong thoughts with the truth of God's Word.

Somebody has said that our thoughts are like rambunctious children who have to be brought under control. That's what Paul had in mind in 2 Corinthians 10:5 when he said, "We are taking every thought captive to the obedience of Christ." God's Word allows us to identify those wrong thoughts, subdue them, and eventually dismiss them.

Jesus: Temptations in the Wilderness

The preeminent example of someone who trusted His training is Jesus, who, though being God, still guarded His soul by committing the words of Scripture to memory. Luke 4:1–2 tells us that at the beginning of Jesus's earthly ministry, the Holy Spirit led Him into the wilderness, where He fasted and faced Satan's temptations for forty days.

On the fortieth day, when Jesus was weak physically and vulnerable spiritually, Satan came to Him with three final temptations. Keep in mind that Jesus didn't have a physical copy of Scripture with Him in the desert. But Jesus carried the words of the Bible in His heart. And by withdrawing the Word of God from His memory bank, Jesus rebuffed Satan's temptations.

The First Temptation: An Appeal to Physical Appetites

After forty days without food, anybody would get hungry—even the Son of God. I sometimes hear people jokingly say, when offered something forbidden on their diet, "Don't tempt me." That's not the kind of temptation Jesus experienced when "the devil said to Him, 'If You are the Son of God, tell this stone to become bread'" (v. 3).

Of course, it's not a sin for a hungry person to eat. Satan's temptation was more sinister than that. Satan was suggesting that after forty days, God had abandoned Jesus by not providing for His physical needs. Therefore, Jesus should satisfy His appetites apart from God.

Now, Jesus was able to turn water into wine, so there was no question that He had the authority and power to turn a rock into a loaf of bread. The point of Satan's temptation was not to test whether Jesus *could* perform the miracle. The temptation was to see if Jesus *would* perform the miracle and feed Himself because He no longer trusted His Father to provide for His needs.

Yet Jesus rejected the notion that God had forgotten Him. Reciting Deuteronomy 8:3 from memory, Jesus said to Satan, "Man shall not live on bread alone" (Luke 4:4). Deuteronomy 8:3 was God's reminder to the Israelites that as they wandered in the wilderness, God would provide for them. He delivered on His promise by daily providing them the gift of manna.

The Second Temptation: An Appeal to Power

In the second temptation, Satan suggested to Jesus that He could fulfill His role as King without having to go to the cross; instead, He could receive the crown from Satan. There was only one catch: Jesus would have to bow down and worship Satan instead of God.

Satan "showed Him all the kingdoms of the world in a moment of time." Then he said to Jesus, "I will give You all this domain and its glory; for it has been handed over to me, and I give it to whomever I wish. Therefore if You worship before me, it shall all be Yours" (vv. 5–7).

Now, you may be wondering, "Pastor, what do you mean that the world has been 'handed over' to Satan? Doesn't the Bible say that God is in control of everything?" Yes, our sovereign God is ultimately in control of everything in the universe. But the Bible also teaches that Satan has been given temporary authority and influence over the world and therefore could make a legitimate offer to Jesus.

As God's Son, Jesus has been promised an earthly kingdom. In Psalm 2:8, the psalmist penned God's promise to the coming

Messiah: "Ask of Me, and I will surely give the nations as Your inheritance, and the very ends of the earth as Your possession." And Daniel's vision of the Son of Man confirmed the extent of Jesus's kingdom: "To Him was given dominion, glory and a kingdom, that all the peoples, nations and men of every language might serve Him. His dominion is an everlasting dominion which will not pass away; and His kingdom is one which will not be destroyed" (Dan. 7:14). So the question that Satan was putting to Jesus essentially was this: "Jesus, will You avoid crucifixion and seize power now by aligning with me? Or will You be obedient to God, go to the cross, and wait until He crowns You King of kings and Lord of lords?"

Jesus again refused Satan's offer. Reciting Deuteronomy 6:13 from memory, Jesus said to Satan, "You shall worship the Lord your God and serve Him only" (Luke 4:8). Jesus was quoting from the traditional Hebrew confession of faith called the Shema ("hear" in Hebrew). This passage is one of the greatest teachings in the Bible.

> Hear, O Israel! The LORD is our God, the LORD is one! You shall love the LORD your God with all your heart and with all your soul and with all your might. These words, which I am commanding you today, shall be on your heart. You shall teach them diligently to your sons and shall talk of them when you sit in your house and when you walk by the way and when you lie down and when you rise up. You shall bind them as a sign on your hand and they shall be as frontals on your forehead. You shall write them on the doorposts of your house and on your gates. (Deut. 6:4–9)

Before the Israelites entered the promised land, the Lord instructed His people to teach their children that there is one

God and that He alone is to be loved and worshiped. They were to pass down their spiritual training from generation to generation by memorizing God's Word, discussing God's Word, and displaying God's Word.

Jesus's spiritual training had kicked in. He would worship God alone. And God would reward Him with power and a kingdom when the time was right.

The Third Temptation: An Appeal to Glory

Up to this point, Jesus had resisted temptation by recalling passages from the Bible to meet Satan's specific attack. But two can play that game. Satan also has the Bible memorized, and he used it in his third temptation—an attempt to convince Jesus to put God to the test.

Leading Jesus to Jerusalem, Satan "had Him stand on the pinnacle of the temple, and said to Him, 'If You are the Son of God, throw Yourself down from here'" (Luke 4:9). Then, quoting Psalm 91:11–12, Satan said, "'He will command His angels concerning You to guard You . . . on their hands they will bear You up, so that You will not strike Your foot against a stone'" (vv. 10–11).

This temptation was an attempt to get Jesus to thwart His mission, which was to go to the cross to atone for our sins. But Satan deliberately misquoted Psalm 91:11 by deleting a crucial phrase. The verse actually reads like this: "He will give His angels charge concerning you to guard you *in all your ways*." Satan attempted to apply that verse to something that would be contrary to God's ways. But Jesus resisted the temptation. He refused to test God by throwing Himself off the temple—which would have summoned the angels to guard Him and thus prove He was the Messiah—because the test would have called into question God's goodness.

Reciting Deuteronomy 6:16 from memory, Jesus said, "You shall not put the Lord your God to the test" (v. 12). Jesus refused to demand miraculous protection where none was needed. Realizing that he had been defeated, Satan departed.

A Training Program for Scripture Memory

Over the years, I have memorized many sections of Scripture. And it's amazing that even though I memorized some of these Scripture passages ten, twenty, or even thirty years ago, they still come back to my mind at the right time. If you want to be prepared to face whatever struggles come your way in life, I encourage you too to make Scripture memory a part of your spiritual routine. Let's look at six ideas to get your training program underway.

Have a Scheduled Time and Plan for Memorizing Scripture

Pick a time when you are mentally alert. If you're a morning person, then set aside time in the morning. If you're an evening person, then choose a time in the evening. No matter what the time of day, set a regular appointment to meet with God. The key is to select the time that is best for you, when you are free from distractions.

Some people like to do this over a cup of coffee at the dining room table. I do this while kneeling beside the couch in my office. If you are unaccustomed to Scripture memorization, don't try to overdo it. Ten or fifteen minutes a day is a great way to start memorizing a verse or two!

There are several practical tools you can use to help you with memorizing Scripture. You can use the Navigators' Topical Memory System, which is a series of verse cards you can take around with you and memorize them. Or, for those of you who read electronically, you can use a Bible memory verse app for your smartphone or tablet. Whatever learning method you use, committing Scripture to memory is an effective way to train yourself for any circumstances you may face.

The important thing is to start. Not long ago, I came across an interesting insight from actor Jeff Bridges about developing good habits. In an interview for *Rolling Stone*, Bridges was asked what advice he wished he would have received at age twenty. The Academy Award–winning actor said, "I got the advice—I just didn't take it! My dad would say, 'It's all about habit, Jeff. You gotta get into good habits.' And I said, 'No, Dad, you gotta live each moment. Live it as the first one and be fresh.' And he says, 'That's a wonderful thought, but that's not what we are. We are habitual creatures. It's about developing these grooves.' As I age, I can see his point. What you practice, that's what you become."[9]

"What you practice, that's what you become." That sage advice applies to every area of life. Perhaps that is why the Bible repeatedly admonishes us to "practice righteousness." We saw in chapter 3 that the term *righteousness* is used in Scripture to refer to our "right standing" with God that we trust in Christ for salvation. But *righteousness* is also used to refer to our obedience to God's commands. The first kind of righteousness (our right standing before God) is the result of

God's grace. The second kind of righteousness (our "right living") is the result of our actions.

And that second kind of righteousness requires hard work. Yet, the hard work gets easier the more we "practice," which explains why the Bible emphasizes practicing righteousness:

> Now for this very reason also, applying all diligence, in your faith supply moral excellence, and in your moral excellence, knowledge, and in your knowledge, self-control. . . . For as long as you *practice* these things, you will never stumble. (2 Pet. 1:5–6, 10)

> By this the children of God, and the children of the devil are obvious: anyone who does not *practice* righteousness is not of God, nor the one who does not love his brother. (1 John 3:10)

> Let the one who does wrong, still do wrong; and the one who is filthy, still be filthy; and let the one who is righteous, still *practice* righteousness; and the one who is holy, still keep himself holy. (Rev. 22:11)

Practicing the habit of Scripture reading and memory is an essential step for the ultimate goal of "practicing" obedience to God. And as you continue to practice obedience, you will develop deep "grooves" that will help you become more like Jesus Christ in every area of your life.

Start Small

When people have been physically malnourished, they don't gorge themselves by eating a sixty-four-ounce steak in one sitting. They begin a little bit at a time. And it is the same way with reading God's Word. If you are suffering from spiritual malnourishment because you have not been feeding regularly on God's Word, then I encourage you to start small. Read a psalm or a proverb. Or read a paragraph from one of the practical books in the New Testament, such as Philippians or James.

You might want to memorize verses according to topic. If you're facing a crisis, try Psalm 46. If you're tempted to sin, look at Psalm 139. If you're lonely or fearful, find comfort in Psalm 27. If you're planning a budget, consult Luke 19. If you're weighed down by responsibilities, let Joshua 1 lift your load.

As you work through the Bible passage you have selected, you will experience this spiritual reality: the more you read God's Word, the more hunger you develop for God's Word.

Read the Verse(s) Out Loud

One of the best ways to memorize Scripture is to engage your vocal cords. In my experience, I have discovered that committing verses to memory is much easier if the process includes not only my eyes but also my tongue and mouth. That way, the words enter my brain through my ears as well.

I encourage you to memorize verses word for word—exactly as written—including the reference. If you break down the verses into independent clauses or phrases and recite the reference as you work on each section, then you'll lock the reference, as well as the verses, into your memory bank.

Another effective way to memorize Scripture by engaging your ears is to set the verses to music. One of my greatest joys as a grandfather is being able to take care of my grand-children while my daughter and her husband enjoy some much-needed time together. The other night, while Amy and I were playing with our grandkids, I sang some children's Bible songs to entertain them. I was surprised by how many Bible verse songs I still remember—more than six decades after I learned them in Sunday school as a child! Many of the Scripture verses I know by heart are ones that were set to music.

Write Out the Verse(s) Word for Word

Another tried-and-true method of memorization is to write out the verses you're working on. Some people are visual learners who benefit from seeing the words, and others are kinesthetic learners who learn by using their hands and sense of touch. Both learning styles benefit from the hands-on activity of writing out verses to memorize them.

I sometimes write out verses on note cards so I can take them with me and review them whenever I can. I know others who write verses on sticky notes and put them on their bathroom mirror or computer. Wherever you choose to write your verses, I suggest placing them somewhere where you will see the words regularly as you learn and then review them.

Underline Difficult or Key Words and Phrases

Underlining key words is helpful if you keep forgetting a word or can't remember the order of the words. For example, let's say you're trying to memorize Matthew 7:7–8: "Ask, and it will be given to you; seek, and you will find; knock, and it will be opened to you. For everyone who asks receives, and he who seeks finds, and to him who knocks it will be opened."

Can you keep "ask," "seek," "knock" in order? If not, underline the first letters of each word and you get A-S-K. That's the order: "ask," "seek," "knock"—ASK.

Draw a Picture Depicting the Verse(s)

Not everyone is a word person; many people prefer pictures and art. If that's you, then you can draw a picture to represent the verse. For example, for Psalm 119:105 you might draw a lamp or flashlight beside some feet. Or for Psalm 119:11 you might draw a heart with a Bible inside it. It doesn't have to be the *Mona Lisa*, but sketch something that depicts the verses you are trying to memorize.

Now, let me give you a word of warning: *always check the context of the verses you are memorizing.* Not every promise or command in the Bible is for us today. Many verses are specific to Israel or the immediate audience. We don't want to memorize a passage and claim the promise or obey the command simply because it's in the Bible. If we're not careful, we might, for example, put this verse as our Christmas card greeting: "Those who dwell on the earth will rejoice over them and celebrate; and they will send gifts to one another" (Rev. 11:10). Why should we not use that verse? Because the context concerns the death of God's two witnesses during the tribulation, and those who are celebrating and giving gifts are the murderers!

Finally, keep in mind that just because someone in the Bible did something doesn't mean we should automatically follow in his or her footsteps. If we believe that every command in Scripture applies to us, regardless of context, then it could have tragic consequences.

This reminds me of the man whose method of studying God's Word was simply to open his Bible, point to a verse, and do whatever it said. One day, he was struggling with a particular decision, so he grabbed his Bible and let the pages fall open. He closed his eyes and pointed to a verse: "[Judas] went away and hanged himself" (Matt. 27:5). *Surely that can't be what God wants me to do*, the man thought. He quickly closed his Bible and then opened it again. Warily, he closed his eyes and pointed to another random verse: "Go and do the same" (Luke 10:37). Startled, the man thought, *I guess the third time's a charm!* Imagine his dismay when he opened his Bible and his finger fell on John 13:27: "What you do, do quickly."

Instead of doing a scavenger hunt for random Bible verses and them trying to apply them to our lives, it is essential to study and understand the context of the verses we are memorizing.

A Deposit That Still Produces Dividends

A few years ago, I was going through some of my old things, and I found my very first bankbook from an account at the Hillcrest State Bank that I opened when I was seven years old. As I reviewed the deposits I made from various odd jobs and gigs playing my accordion, I noticed that on May 29, 1975, I withdrew all the money from that bank account—and I don't have a clue where it went. All those deposits I made were gone.

But there is one deposit I've made through the years that continues to pay dividends in my life. It's the deposit of God's Word that I've put into my heart. I can recall moments of temptation or discouragement when God brought to my mind specific passages of Scripture I had committed to memory that kept me from crashing my life—and destroying the lives of those "on board" with me.

In Deuteronomy 32:46–47, Moses said to the Israelites, "Take to your heart all the words with which I am warning you today, which you shall command your sons to observe carefully, even all the words of this law. For it is not an idle word for you; indeed it is your life." God's Word is our life, and it holds the only hope for surviving the unseen but very real forces at work to destroy us.

The goal of Scripture memorization is not to see how many verses you can master but to be mastered by the verses you have memorized. That way, when you enter the inevitable turbulence that life produces, you will be able to let your training take over until you can safely land.

Bend, Don't Break

In his Nobel Prize–winning novel, *The Old Man and the Sea*, Ernest Hemingway told the story of a Cuban deep-sea fisherman who landed a marlin in a skiff—a canoe-shaped open boat. Fishing in deep waters for large fish, in a boat that is just twenty-five feet long and sits low in the water, is a dangerous undertaking. But fishermen in Latin America still use skiffs in the Caribbean Sea, the Gulf of Mexico, and the Pacific Ocean.

One such fisherman, Salvador Alvarenga, discovered just how dangerous it could be.

Setting out from Mexico on November 18, 2012, Alvarenga, along with his fishing companion, Ezequiel Córdoba, fired up the motor on his skiff and surfed over the crashing waves of the Pacific Ocean that came rolling onto the beach. His boat was weighed down with a thousand pounds of fishing equipment, including a five-by-four-foot icebox that he hoped to fill with tuna, shark, and mahi-mahi. Though Alvarenga was aware of approaching storms, he ignored the warnings. He calculated that one day of good fishing would net him enough money to live on for an entire week. To him, that was worth the gamble.

When they were about seventy-five miles offshore, Alvarenga and Córdoba began to let out their two-mile-long fishing line. The seas were calm—until around one in the morning. Then the wind picked up. Waves began crashing over the sides of the boat, filling it with water. Alvarenga tried to pull in the fishing line, but more water was coming over the sides than Córdoba could bail out. Alvarenga had no choice: he had to cut the line and race toward home.

With dawn approaching, Alvarenga and Córdoba could see mountains on the horizon. Then the motor coughed . . . and died. Alvarenga yanked on the cord. Nothing. He yanked again, but this time the cord broke. As the ocean raised and dropped the skiff, the two men saw the mountains disappear as the boat floated away from shore.

The storm raged for five days. After constant bailing, both men were exhausted. They had drifted some 280 miles from the Mexican shoreline. Rescue seemed nearly impossible. Since the skiff sat so low in the water, it would be extremely difficult for anyone to spot it. And they had no flare gun or other means to call for help. They were at the mercy of the sea.

The sun baked their skin during the day, and to fend off the cold at night, Alvarenga and Córdoba climbed into the icebox for warmth. Finding fresh water was an immediate concern. Thankfully, a few days after the storm, it rained again. The men laid out plastic bottles they had scavenged from the ocean and collected about five gallons of fresh water.

Eleven days into their ordeal, after having survived on bony triggerfish caught by hand, Alvarenga was able to catch a sea turtle. In hopes of raising his friend's spirits, Alvarenga decided to present the turtle meat as a delicacy. He cut the meat into thin strips, dipped them in sea water for flavor, and toasted them in the sun on the outboard motor. Using the vertebrae of the triggerfish as toothpicks, Alvarenga served the meat on the turtle shell.

Eating what they could catch by hand from the sea, and the occasional seabird that landed on the skiff, was just enough to stave off starvation as days turned into weeks and weeks turned into months. Alvarenga established a routine to keep himself and Córdoba alive. Alvarenga was always awake by 5:00 a.m., checking the traps he had put out the night before. To escape the brutal sun, they climbed in the icebox. At night, they laid face-up and drew doodles in the sky.

Then things went from bad to worse. One evening, the two men ate a seabird. Córdoba soon grabbed his stomach and frothed at the mouth. Inspecting the bird, they discovered it had eaten a poisonous snake. Though Córdoba's stomach got better, he never recovered psychologically. Within a couple of months, Córdoba had physically shriveled up. "Goodbye, Chancha," Córdoba said, using Alvarenga's nickname, and began to throw himself over the side of the skiff. Alvarenga caught him, wrestled him into the icebox, and sat down on the lid. When Córdoba calmed down, Alvarenga laid down next to his friend. "We have to fight. To tell our story," he said.

But it was too late. Córdoba died a few days later.

With the death of his friend, Alvarenga concentrated on keeping himself occupied. He hunted turtles and seabirds.

He trapped fish. And he designed a shark-detection system that permitted him to take short swims to wash and cool himself. What got him through the lonely hours, however, was the thought of his daughter and the growing sense that the Lord must have some reason for his life.

Then on January 30, 2014—after more than a year afloat in the skiff—Alvarenga noticed coconuts bobbing in the water and shorebirds filling the sky. In the distance, he could just make out a tiny island. When he was about ten yards from shore, Alvarenga dove into the sea and let the waves carry him to shore, gripping "a handful of sand . . . like it was a treasure." He had washed ashore on the Ebon Atoll, the southern tip of the Marshall Islands, one of the most remote spots on the globe. Had he missed this tiny speck of land, the next likely stop was the Philippines, three thousand miles away.[1]

Bend, Don't Break

"The wind doesn't break a tree that bends," an African proverb says. And Alvarenga chose to bend. Whether it was through his daily routine, his game of connecting the stars with Córdoba, or thinking about his daughter, he was determined to survive.

Salvador Alvarenga demonstrated not only the will to survive but also resilience. Resilience is the trait of being able to return to an original shape after being twisted, compressed, or stretched. Survivalists use the term to refer to the ability to pick oneself up after a setback, dust off, and continue to move forward.

As followers of Jesus Christ, we need to develop the ability to bend and not break in a culture that is drifting further and further from God. Now, perhaps more than ever, we need to stand firm in our Christian convictions. But *how* we maintain our convictions is just as important as our convictions themselves. For example, it's one thing for the *message* of the gospel to be a stumbling block to people coming to faith in Christ; it's something quite different for the *messengers* of the gospel to be a stumbling block.

When it comes to living courageously in a hostile world, striking the balance of bending—and not breaking—can be a tricky one. Fortunately, Paul's admonishment in Romans 12 and Daniel's example in Babylon give us practical lessons in finding that balance.

How to Handle Opposition

It was unwise for Alvarenga to venture into a hostile environment despite repeated warnings of impending storms. But you and I don't have any choice about living in a culture that is increasingly hostile toward God and His truth. Isolation is not an option . . . or even a possibility. And it's not God's will for us either.

In John 17:15, Jesus prayed for all His future followers, including you and me: "I do not ask You to take them out of the world, but to keep them from the evil one." To prevent Satan from turning us into spiritual roadkill, we need to be aware of the challenges that inevitably face those who choose to remain faithful in a world that is opposed to the ways of Christ. But, like Alvarenga, our capacity to flex and bend with uncontrollable variables can be the key to surviving difficult times.

On the night He was betrayed, Jesus said to His disciples, "If the world hates you, you know that it has hated Me before it hated you. If you were of the world, the world would love its own; but because you are not of the world, but I chose you out of the world, because of this the world hates you. . . . If they persecuted Me, they will also persecute you" (15:18–20).

In the following chapter, Jesus warned His disciples, "In the world you have tribulation" (16:33). It was true then, and it is true now. If you follow the news, you've seen stories of Christian photographers, florists, and bakers who have been sued and/or fined for refusing to participate in same-sex weddings. The people who are bringing suit claim these Christian tradespeople violated the human rights of same-sex couples. What is misunderstood, or simply ignored, is the counterclaim that for Christians to participate in these weddings would violate their religious convictions by endorsing relationships prohibited by Scripture. The question in these instances is whether the right of religious liberty must be surrendered for the "right" of personal preference.

But we don't have to look to the culture at large to find hostility toward Christians. Chances are you have a coworker, neighbor, or family member who opposes your Christian convictions. You've seen their snide comments on social media. Or perhaps they seem to go out of their way to use the Lord's name in vain in your presence. Not long ago, a friend told me that his homosexual cousin effectively cut off all contact with him because the cousin doesn't want anything to do with his Christian beliefs.

How are we to respond to such opposition to our faith? How can we have the courage to bend and not break? Paul offered some advice in Romans 12:17–21:

> Never pay back evil for evil to anyone. Respect what is right in the sight of all men. If possible, so far as it depends on you, be at peace with all men. Never take your own revenge, beloved, but leave room for the wrath of God, for it is written, "Vengeance is Mine, I will repay," says the Lord. "But if your enemy is hungry, feed him, and if he is thirsty, give him a drink; for in so doing you will heap burning coals on his head." Do not be overcome by evil, but overcome evil with good.

Paul opened Romans 12 by urging believers to sacrifice our human desires for God's desires. He then admonished us not to be molded into the ways of the world, which would only encourage our natural desires. Rather, we are to be transformed by training our minds to think about the ways of God.

If there was ever a time when Christians should deny what is natural and do what is supernatural, it's when we face opposition for our faith. No matter how great the antagonism, Paul was clear: we are not to seek vengeance. On the contrary, Paul said we ought to "bless those who persecute [us]; bless and do not curse" (v. 14). Our natural instinct is to lash out—to "pay back evil for evil" (v. 17), but Paul told us to do what is supernatural: "bless and do not curse."

The Greek word for "bless" means "to speak well of" or "to praise." When we bless instead of curse, we fulfill the second half of Romans 12:17: "Respect what is right in the sight of all men." The Greek word for "respect" means looking past offenses to see what good we can do, even for those who persecute us. It means maintaining Christlike attitudes

live through it
Be a light through it

and behavior that even our enemies recognize as upstanding. In short, it is living truthful and honorable lives.

Nevertheless, Paul was a realist. He knew that some people would never be won over, no matter how respectfully we respond to them. Bullies are a dime a dozen. That's why Paul said, "*If it is possible, as far as it depends on you*, live at peace with everyone" (v. 18 NIV).

Let me be clear: this verse should not be interpreted as peace at any price. Sometimes the price of peace is too high, especially when truth is at stake. Even Jesus Christ—the Prince of Peace—chose truth over peace when it came to the gospel message. He said, "Do not think that I came to bring peace on the earth; I did not come to bring peace, but a sword. For I came to set a man against his father, and a daughter against her mother, and a daughter-in-law against her mother-in-law" (Matt. 10:34–35).

But whenever possible and appropriate, the responsibility of pursuing peace sits squarely on the shoulders of Christians.

Dos and Don'ts of Peacemaking

How are we to pursue peace, especially with those whom we consider enemies? Paul offers a list of dos and don'ts that every peacemaker should follow.

Peacemakers Don't Take Their Own Revenge

First, peacemakers don't take their own revenge. Paul wrote, "Never take your own revenge, beloved, but leave room for the wrath of God, for it is written, 'Vengeance is Mine, I will repay,' says the Lord" (Rom. 12:19). When someone deliberately causes us harm, we are to turn the other cheek, as Jesus said in Matthew 5:39. An enemy isn't won over through confrontation. Proverbs 15:1 says, "A harsh word stirs up anger." Sometimes it's better to walk away and choose not to assert our rights. When we do this, Paul said, we "leave room" for God to champion our cause (Rom. 12:19).

It's important to note two things about Paul's command not to take our own revenge. First, Paul is talking about personal offenses, not spiritual convictions. Some Christians condemned Colorado baker Jack Philipps for refusing to design a cake for a gay wedding. "Why not surrender your right not to make the cake in order to show Christ's love to others?" they asked. But Philipps could not surrender God's truth that marriage is between a man and a woman, nor could he surrender his conviction that to do so would violate his conscience.

Second, refraining from taking our own revenge does not exempt us from seeking justice. Revenge is attempting to hurt somebody for hurting us. On the other hand, justice is allowing God or others to right the wrongs committed against us. Even the apostle Paul himself spent two years seeking justice through the Roman legal system for the violation of his rights as a Roman citizen. Seeking justice from law enforcement or the legal system for offenses against us can be one way to "leave room for the wrath of God."

However, even when our cause is just, our goal is not to pound our enemies into the ground but to redeem them, turning them into allies and friends, if at all possible. Jesus is the perfect illustration of what Romans 12:19 looks like in action. Peter described it well: "While being reviled, He did not revile in return; while suffering, He uttered no threats, but kept entrusting Himself to Him who judges righteously" (1 Pet. 2:23).

When I think of somebody who embodied the spirit of Romans 12:19, I think of Martin Luther King Jr. and his nonviolent resistance against a corrupt political system. He fought for greater civil freedoms, but he did so without vengeance. Instead, he used persuasion, compassion, and love. Speaking to the Southern Christian Leadership Conference a year before his assassination, King said, "I have decided to stick to love. . . . Hate is too great a burden to bear."[2] Like King, we are to defend the weak and pursue justice. This is our biblical mandate. But we are never to seek retaliation for personal insults or slights.

Peacemakers Seek the Good of Their Enemies

The second way to be a peacemaker, according to the apostle Paul, is to seek the good of our enemies. We are to be hospitable to those who offend us. This is the point Paul made in Romans 12:20–21: "'If your enemy is hungry, feed him, and if he is thirsty, give him a drink; for in so doing you will heap burning coals on his head.' Do not be overcome by evil, but overcome evil with good."

You may be wondering, *Why would I want to do something good for my enemy?* Notice the two reasons Paul gives us for doing good to our enemies. First of all, it will bring conviction to your enemy. "In so doing you will heap burning coals on his head" (v. 20). Now, I have read every convoluted interpretation of that phrase you can imagine. And there are some pretty crazy interpretations. Some people, for example, say, "What this means is if your enemy's fire went out, the most loving thing you could do would be to give him some burning coals so he could restart his fire. When you gave him those burning coals, he would put them in a container and carry them on top of his head." But that's not what Paul was saying here.

Other people say, "Well, 'heap burning coals on his head' means that when you do good to your enemy, you are inflicting great pain because you're making him feel guilty, so it's a win-win for you. You get to watch your enemy writhe in pain, and you get credit with God for doing something good. It's the best of both worlds." Is that what Paul was saying? No, this isn't some back door to revenge.

I think Paul was saying that when you do good to your enemy, you are giving him what he really needs, and that is conviction. That is, your enemy does feel pain when you don't respond as he thinks you're going to respond—when you do good for him instead of retaliating. But that conviction, that pain, leads your enemy to repent and turn to God. So by doing good to your enemy, you are giving him what he needs most: repentance that leads to salvation.

This reminds me of the story of Peter Miller, a Baptist minister who lived in Ephrata, Pennsylvania, during the Revolutionary War. Pastor Miller was regularly harassed and humiliated by his mean-spirited neighbor, Michael Wittman. But when Miller heard that Wittman had been arrested for treason and sentenced to death, he walked seventy miles to Philadelphia to ask his friend George Washington to spare the life of the traitor.

General Washington said, "No, Peter. I cannot grant you the life of your friend."

"My friend!" said the pastor. "He is the bitterest enemy I have."

"What?" exclaimed Washington. "You have walked all these miles to save the life of an enemy? That puts the matter in different light. I will grant your pardon."

Peter Miller returned home with the pardoned Michael Wittman, who was no longer his enemy but his friend.[3]

Miller is an example of someone who understood Paul's admonition to "heap burning coals" upon an enemy's head by showing him kindness—an action that resulted in bringing his former enemy to repentance.

Paul wrapped up his teaching on how to handle opposition with a summary statement: "Do not be overcome by evil, but overcome evil with good" (v. 21). This is the gospel message in one simple sentence. God's purpose in the death and resurrection of His Son is to extinguish evil with the good news of Jesus Christ. When we respond to enemies by refusing to retaliate and by striving toward peace, we are a living demonstration of the gospel.

Daniel: A Man Who Chose to Bend but Not Break

No person in the Bible better illustrates the principle of bending but not breaking when under fire than the Old Testament character Daniel. Forcibly removed from his homeland by the Babylonians, Daniel was thrown into that pagan culture and ordered to conform, which would have violated his religious convictions. However, instead of openly defying the authorities, Daniel courageously found a way to bend and, in doing so, won the praise of God and his captors.

Daniel was likely a teenager when Babylon took him captive in 605 BC. Based on his actions recorded in the book that bears his name, Daniel must have been taught to honor God and the Scriptures early in life. It was that obedience, along with God's guidance and grace, that eventually elevated Daniel to a position of prominence in Babylon. But first, he had to undergo a grueling reeducation program designed to strip him of his personal, ethnic, and religious identity.

Having acquired the new territory of Judah, King Nebuchadnezzar needed bright young men to administer Jewish affairs. He ordered Ashpenaz, "the chief of his officials," to select the best from the "sons of Israel, including some of the royal family and of the nobles" (Dan. 1:3). The young men selected were between the ages of thirteen and nineteen, without disabilities or ailments, and physically attractive. They were also intelligent, practical, and well versed in the ways of nobility. These young men would be trained to serve "in the king's court" (v. 4).

Once Ashpenaz made his selections, he put these young men through a rigorous three-year program of mastering the Babylonian language and practices. Immersed in a pagan culture, alienated from the Word of God, and forbidden to speak Hebrew, these teenagers were easy prey for indoctrination into the idolatry around them. If anything could fracture their spiritual resolve, this program would surely do it.

Learning Babylonian ways was one thing, but being stripped of his identity was another. Daniel's Hebrew name—meaning "God is my Judge"—reflected the greatness of God. So Daniel was given a Babylonian name, "Belteshazzar" (v. 7). Extolling the greatness of Bel, a pagan deity, Daniel's new name meant, "May Bel protect his life."

For three years, Daniel received one of the best educations in the ancient world. After graduation, he would be assured an influential position in the Babylonian government. All he had to do was deny his language, his identity, and his religion.

Daniel had already lost his family, his freedom, and his country, as well as his personal and ethnic identity. The Babylonians, however, also sought to corrupt his commitment to God and His Word. Daniel and the other young men were to be served food and wine from the king's own table. There was just one problem: much of the king's food violated God's standards in the law. For the Hebrew young men to eat the Babylonian delicacies would be to break God's law and honor a pagan god.

Daniel couldn't do much about the fact that he was a captive or was given a new name. But he could do something about whether he would violate his conscience. So he resolved that "he would not defile himself" with the king's food (v. 8).

This is where we see Daniel bend and not break. He could have refused to eat the king's food and suffered the consequences, which would have been death. Instead, Daniel approached Ashpenaz and reasoned with him, seeking "permission . . . not [to] defile himself," which moved Ashpenaz's heart with "favor and compassion" (vv. 8–9). However, Ashpenaz feared that if Daniel didn't eat the king's food, he wouldn't look as healthy as the other young men. Ashpenaz knew he would get blamed for failing to look after Daniel properly.

Sensitive to his captor's dilemma, Daniel proposed a test. He and his friends would eat nothing but vegetables and drink nothing but water for ten days. At the end of that time, if Daniel and his friends didn't look better than the other young men, then they would concede to eating and drinking from the king's table. And wouldn't you know it, after ten days of vegetables and water, "their appearance seemed better and they were fatter than all the youths who had been eating the king's choice food" (v. 15). Wisely, Ashpenaz continued to allow Daniel's strict vegetarian diet.

Because Daniel refused to compromise his convictions and chose to trust God, the Lord blessed him with knowledge, intelligence, and the ability to understand "all kinds of visions and dreams" (v. 17). The people around Daniel recognized his wisdom and insight, and Nebuchadnezzar was so impressed that he made Daniel a personal counselor.

How to Bend without Breaking

Even as a teenager, Daniel demonstrated resilience. He could accept a Babylonian education and a new name, but he refused to compromise his deepest convictions. Yet he was wise enough to find a way to bend instead of break. Daniel could have stormed into the palace and said to Nebuchadnezzar, "You pagan king! I can't believe you would suggest that I defile myself by breaking God's law." Had he done so, he doubtlessly would have been the first Hebrew martyr in Babylon! While that distinction might have been admirable, Daniel would have forfeited the ministry that God had planned for him in Babylon for the next seventy years.

Fortunately, Daniel chose to display the wisdom and discernment that had made the king notice him in the first place. Daniel demonstrated his respect for the king's office and presented his request politely. The result not only led to favor in the sight of God and others but also led to peace. As Proverbs 16:7 says, "When a man's ways are pleasing to the LORD, He makes even his enemies to be at peace with him."

How can we experience a similar outcome as we seek to live Christianly in a culture that is becoming increasingly anti-Christian? I have two suggestions, based on what we have seen from Romans 12 and Daniel's life.

Be a Winsome Witness

Do you know who the least hypocritical people in the world are? Sinning sinners. When they sin, they are merely doing what comes naturally to them. Sinners sin; it's that simple. But I meet Christians all the time who are surprised—or angered—for example, when Hollywood produces another movie filled with filth. The truth is, there's no reason to get upset when sinners sin. What do you expect them to do? When people don't know the freedom that comes from a relationship with Jesus Christ, they are slaves to sin. So they sin.

What ought to shock us is when Christians sin. There is nothing more hypocritical than when a person who has the indwelling power of the Holy Spirit breaks under the pressure of temptation. Yet we do it all the time. And when we do, we damage our Christian witness. That's why, in the previous chapter, we talked about how important it is to memorize Scripture. It's our only sure defense against temptation.

Keeping ourselves free from sin, though, is only one way to be a winsome witness. The other is living out our biblical convictions with joy and grace. Christians today are standing courageously against those who deliberately—or sometimes innocently—attempt to take away our constitutional rights and impede our biblical mandate to spread the message of Jesus Christ. But in doing so, we don't have to act like jerks!

In my book *Twilight's Last Gleaming*, I told of a time when my family chose to be a winsome witness. When my older daughter was in elementary school, she came home one day and told me about a friend who was stopped by the principal for passing out water bottles labeled with John 4:14: "Whoever drinks of the water that I will give him shall never thirst." The principal, who was a committed Christian, told the student that passing out bottles labeled with a Bible verse violated the separation of church and state.

My daughter asked, "Dad, can he do that?" "No," I explained to her. "The First Amendment of the Constitution guarantees our right to express our faith." I decided that for the sake of the gospel, as well as an example to my daughter of standing up for truth, I needed to talk to the principal. First, I called my friend Kelly Shackleford of the Liberty Legal Institute, which champions the rights of Christians, to get the latest court rulings about this issue.

Once armed with the facts, I called the principal. First, I expressed my appreciation for all he had done for my daughters. I then acknowledged the difficult spot he was in as a Christian principal in a public school. Finally, I explained that while he probably thought he was doing his job by prohibiting distribution of the water bottles, he was actually violating the student's rights—something I was sure he would not want to do. He thanked me for making him aware of the facts and reversed his position.

I realize this incident does not qualify as a landmark legal victory. However, in one small corner of Texas, a young girl's constitutional rights were preserved and her efforts to spread the gospel were unfettered by a firm but courteous stand for truth. Think what would happen if every follower of Christ around the world would graciously but boldly push back against attempts to neutralize Christianity's influence on our culture![4]

Now, we don't have to dump a truckload of Bible verses on people in an effort to get them right with the Lord. Instead, the Bible says, we ought to "lead a tranquil and quiet life in all godliness and dignity. This is good and acceptable in the sight of God our Savior, who desires all men to be saved and to come to the knowledge of the truth" (1 Tim. 2:2–4). God's great longing is that all would come to know the truth of the gospel. He would like to use you in helping fulfill that desire. But that requires you to extend grace to others.

Be a Peacemaker

Someone once joked, "Peace is that brief glorious moment in history when everybody stands around reloading." But that's not peace. Peace isn't an absence of war or hostilities between two enemies still bent on mutual destruction. We call that an armistice. Peace is a sense of rest and well-being between formerly warring parties.

Spiritually speaking, peace is found in trusting in God. Psalm 46:10 says, "Cease striving and know that I am God." Unfortunately, many people today aren't experiencing this peace. Thomas Merton correctly diagnosed the human condition like this: "We are not at peace with others because we are not at peace with ourselves, and we are not at peace with ourselves because we are not at peace with God."[5] So how can we bring peace into our lives and the lives of others? The Bible tells us to become peacemakers.

Now, it's important to understand that *peacemaking* is not the same as *peacekeeping*. Peacekeeping seeks peace from conflict through force of arms. Peacemaking seeks peace in our hearts through forgiveness and reconciliation. Peacemaking begins with God, which is why the beatitude calls those who make peace "children of God" (Matt. 5:9 NIV). To become a peacemaker, we must first become children of God. We do that by faith, believing that Jesus died to forgive our sins and rose from the dead to give us new life. It is only through faith in the death and resurrection of Jesus Christ that God transforms enemies into adopted children.

"I've tried to be at peace with others," you may be saying, "but they don't always want to restore the relationship. And sometimes, they're downright hostile! What should I do if I try to make peace, but the other person doesn't respond?" That's a great question, and the Bible answers it. In Romans 12:18, Paul wrote, "*As far as it depends on you*, live at peace with everyone" (NIV). Scripture is clear that peace is not your responsibility alone. You cannot be responsible for how the other party responds to your peacemaking efforts. And sometimes, when the conflict centers on something that is clearly stated in God's Word, it is impossible to maintain peace with a friend or family member or employer or the government while maintaining your spiritual convictions.

There is only so far we can bend in a culture that is increasingly at odds with God.

How to Say No to the Culture

As our culture becomes more hostile to God and His truth, followers of Jesus will experience times when we are in conflict with the governing authorities. How can we be effective ambassadors for Christ when we are forced to choose between following the culture and following God? Is there ever a time that Christians need to say no to their authorities?

In Scripture, we see that Peter, Paul, and even Jesus Himself lost their lives because they said no to the governing authorities. So clearly there are times when we are to resist authority. Let me share with you three principles we need to consider before we engage in civil disobedience.

Pick Your Battles Carefully

First, if you say no to the government, make sure your disobedience is based on a clear biblical mandate. In Acts 5, Peter and the apostles were boldly proclaiming the gospel, and the Jewish officials commanded them to quit preaching the name of Jesus. "But Peter and the apostles answered, 'We must obey God rather than men'" (v. 29). The command to quit preaching in the name of Jesus was a clear violation of the God-ordained mandate in Acts 1:8. The disciples didn't have to think twice about their civil disobedience in this situation.

But not every government law that has religious overtones necessarily needs to be disobeyed. For example, the government says that if our church wants to retain its tax-exempt status, I, as a pastor, cannot officially endorse a political candidate from the pulpit. Privately, I am free to say and do whatever I want to politically. I can stand in the pulpit and tell you whom I am voting for personally, but I cannot officially endorse a candidate, or our church will lose its tax-exempt status. Now, imagine that I say, "You know what? I am a preacher of the gospel, and I am going to say whatever I want to say." If I do that, then the government will say, "Fine, we are going to yank your church's tax-exempt status." Now, if that happens, I will not be suffering for righteousness's sake; I will be suffering the consequences of my own stupidity. That is not persecution.

There are Christians who say, "I refuse to pay my taxes because I don't agree with the way the money is being used. I don't like my taxes going to support abortion or sexual immorality, so I am going to withhold my money from the government." But Jesus said, "Render to Caesar the things that are Caesar's" (Matt. 22:21). Jesus knew the Roman system would end up killing Him. Yet He said that even when the government is corrupt, you need to pay your taxes. So if people refuse to pay their taxes and end up going to jail, then they are not going for righteousness's sake; they are going for their own dishonesty in not paying their taxes.

Today, some Christians are involved in protesting. Occasionally during their protests, they violate somebody's property rights and get arrested. Again, in that case, their punishment is for disobeying governing authorities, not for the sake of righteousness. When we choose to say no to the government, we need to make sure that the law we are disobeying is a violation of a clear biblical mandate.

Demonstrate Respect for Authority

Second, if you engage in civil disobedience, demonstrate respect for authority when you say no. As we saw previously, Daniel disobeyed the government, but he did so in a respectful way. The king found favor with that idea, and God honored Daniel's choice.

We see the same thing with Peter. After Caiaphas, the Jewish high priest, told Peter and the disciples to quit preaching in the name of Jesus, did Peter respond, "You Christ killer, why would I listen to you? You can go jump in the Sea of Galilee!"? No, he didn't do that. Instead, he respectfully but firmly said, "We must obey God rather than men" (Acts 5:29). I believe in these days, as we see our country moving further and further away from its Christian heritage, we are going to have to say no to government—especially as it begins to abrogate our very real First Amendment rights of free speech and the free exercise of religion. But when we choose to disobey our government for the sake of obeying God, we don't have to act like jerks in doing so. The Bible says we need to act with respect.

Be Prepared to Suffer for Your Convictions

Third, if you engage in civil disobedience, be prepared to suffer the consequences. Some Christians decide to stand boldly for their faith in their workplace, and then they are surprised when they get fired. They say, "Wait a minute, God; this isn't supposed to happen. You are supposed to honor me for my obedience to You." Some people take a stand for Christ and are surprised when they end up in a police station.

They think somehow that if they do the right thing, then at the last moment God is going to exempt them from any kind of suffering. But it doesn't work that way. If indeed you choose to disobey the government, then you need to be ready to suffer the consequences of that disobedience.

When Dr. Martin Luther King Jr. was incarcerated in a Birmingham jail because he led a nonviolent protest against racism, some Christian pastors criticized his civil disobedience. They said, "You should not disobey the government. You ought to fight your battle in the courts and not in the streets." In response to this criticism, Dr. King wrote a letter in which he said:

> One may well ask: "How can you advocate breaking some laws and obeying others?" The answer is found in the fact that there are two types of laws: There are just laws and there are unjust laws. I would be the first to advocate obeying just laws. One has not only a legal but a moral responsibility to obey just laws. Conversely, one has a moral responsibility to disobey unjust laws. . . .
>
> A just law is a man-made code that squares with the moral law or the law of God. An unjust law is a code that is out of harmony with the moral law.[6]

Dr. King believed that any law that codified racial discrimination violated not just the moral law but the law of God, so he said no. He wasn't surprised that he ended up in jail. He didn't complain about his mistreatment. He knew the consequences of civil disobedience. And it will be the same for any of us who say no to the government.

Remember this: most Christians are not spared the consequences of saying no to the government. Daniel had to spend a night with the lions for his disobedience to Darius. The apostle Paul lost his head because he said no to the Roman government. Even Jesus was crucified because He would not renounce that He was the Son of God.

What happened when Peter said to Caiaphas, "We must obey God rather than men" (Acts 5:29)? Did Caiaphas suddenly say, "Peter, you are right, and I am wrong! I don't know why I said such a thing. Go on your way, and I will leave you alone"? Was there a supernatural deliverance? No. Acts 5:40 says, "After calling the apostles in, they flogged them and ordered them not to speak in the name of Jesus, and then released them." Peter and the disciples were beaten because they said no to the government. But what was their response to their suffering? Look at verse 41: "They went on their way from the presence of the Council, rejoicing that they had been considered worthy to suffer shame for His name." They didn't organize a pity party for themselves, moaning, "Oh, poor us! We are suffering for Christ." Instead, they rejoiced that they had the privilege of suffering for the name of Christ.

Does that mean we are not to do anything about the persecution of Christians in our world? When we see our brothers and sisters in Christ around the globe being slaughtered, are we supposed to sit back and say, "What a privilege it is for them to suffer in the name of Christ"? No, we are to stand up against evil. We are to stand up against terrorists and totalitarian regimes that are slaughtering our brothers and sisters in Christ. We are to call on our government officials to use any and every means necessary to put an end to Christian suffering around the world. This is no time for Christians to be silent.

The same thing is true in our country. As we see the beliefs of conservative Christians increasingly being marginalized, as we watch our rights being taken away—our First Amendment rights that our forefathers gave their life's blood for us to have—we are not to stay silent.

Study the example of the apostle Paul. Paul was the greatest missionary and evangelist in the world, yet he spent two years tied up in the Roman legal system fighting for his rights as a Roman citizen to share the message of Jesus Christ. No, we are not to remain silent when persecution comes. But if indeed you suffer for the name of Christ, then rejoice in that. Consider it a privilege that God would allow you to suffer in the name of the One who gave His life for us.

If you prayerfully choose to engage in civil disobedience as you strive to bend but not break in our hostile culture, then remember the promise of Paul in 2 Timothy 2:12: "If we endure, we will also reign with Him."

If we are going to survive, and even thrive, during these challenging days, we must learn to bend and not break. We must learn to practice what we preach without compromising our Christian convictions in an increasingly anti-Christian culture. None of this comes naturally. As I said earlier, putting Romans 12:14, 17–21 into practice is to live supernaturally. Nevertheless, if we bless others who curse us, if we leave room for God to avenge us, and if we seek peace in a creative and grace-filled manner, as Daniel did, then we just might "overcome evil with good."

Beware of Celebrating the Summit

Doug Hansen, a forty-seven-year-old postal worker from Kent, Washington, couldn't afford expert mountain climber Rob Hall's $65,000 fee to guide him up the side of Mount Everest. Unlike the rest of the climbers in the group on his 1996 Everest trek, Hansen had to scrape every penny together to make the trip. He even enlisted the kids at Sunrise Elementary School in his hometown to sell T-shirts to help pay the bill. In return, they would receive postcards from Nepal and, if he successfully summited the mountain, a picture of the school's flag planted on top of Everest.

Hansen had tried to reach the summit of Mount Everest the previous year. But because of Rob Hall's strict turn-around time—a measure used to ensure a safe return to camp before bad weather or nightfall—the guide had turned Hansen back just 330 vertical feet below the summit. Hall felt bad about denying Hansen the crown then, so he offered a reduced rate if Hansen would try again in 1996.

Between the two expeditions, Hansen obsessed about the summit of Everest. Thinking back to his previous expedition, Hansen told fellow '96 Everest climber Jon Krakauer, "The summit looks *sooooo* close. Believe me, there hasn't been a day since that I haven't thought about it."[1]

In the dark hours of May 10, 1996, Hansen, along with Krakauer and the others in Hall's group, left camp in their bid to reach the roof of the world. However, three hours into the climb, Hansen was unable to shake the cold. Feeling miserable, he pulled aside to let others pass him on the rope. He told one of the climbers that the summit would have to wait another year. When Hall reached Hansen, a conversation ensued. No one heard what was said, but Hansen got back on the rope and continued his ascent.

Throughout the day, the climbers began to spread out— stronger climbers raced ahead, and weaker climbers lagged behind. Hall's turnaround time was 2:00 p.m.—a deadline that was to be obeyed without question. Nevertheless, violating his own rule, Hall crested the summit at 2:10. He radioed base camp: "Doug is just coming up over the horizon." But the figure Hall saw wasn't Hansen. He was still two hours from making the summit. According to a Nepalese climbing guide for another expedition, Hansen didn't reach the top until after 4:00, and then only with the help of Hall.

Hall, who had been sitting at the summit—29,035 feet— for two hours, didn't allow Hansen much time to celebrate the accomplishment of his dream. They had to descend fast! But Hansen was out of bottled oxygen and completely spent. At 4:30 and 4:41, Hall radioed that he and Hansen were in trouble and needed oxygen. By this time, an approaching storm was beginning to look ominous. When Hall radioed again, the storm had engulfed the mountain. Sometime between Hall's 5:57 p.m. distress call on May 10 and his call at 4:43 a.m. on May 11, Doug Hansen either slid or stepped off the mountain.[2] About forty-five minutes later, base camp reached Hall on the radio and asked about Hansen. "Doug is gone," Hall said.

Don't Celebrate the Summit

Everyone in the mountaineering community believed Rob Hall's Adventure Consultants was the safest guiding service money could buy. Yet something went terribly wrong on that May afternoon in 1996. Rob Hall violated his own strict turnaround time, and Doug Hansen lost his life. In the end, so did Hall. After enduring a night of windchill 100 degrees below zero, Hall finally succumbed to the extreme environment.

In what became the deadliest season on Everest at the time—twelve people perished before the climbing season ended—many began asking questions. How could this have happened? What was Hall thinking? Why didn't he, after summiting the mountain himself, descend and turn Hansen around instead of waiting two hours for his struggling client to reach the top?

Some said the answer was competition within the mountain-guiding industry. The business model for such endeavors is simple: the more people you get to the top, the more clients you sign; the more clients you sign, the more money you make. Others said it was arrogance—macho men doing macho things. Wherever the truth lies, one thing is certain: the goal of climbing a mountain isn't to reach the summit; it's to make it home *from* the summit.

Mountaineer Jon Krakauer, who summited that day in May, wrote, "Reaching the top of Everest is supposed to trigger a surge of intense elation; against long odds, after all, I had just attained a goal I'd coveted since childhood. But the summit was really only the halfway point. Any impulse I might have felt toward self-congratulation was extinguished by overwhelming apprehension about the long, dangerous descent that lay ahead."[3]

I understand the challenge of the summit, because my own father was an amateur mountain climber. I did not inherit his interest in mountaineering. I have no desire to climb Mount Everest—or any mountain, for that matter. (Just climbing up a stepladder to change a lightbulb makes me a little queasy!) But there is a truth about scaling large mountains that applies to something I am interested in: pursuing and fulfilling dreams.

If we are not careful, we can allow our dreams to consume us and distract us from what is truly important. And when we fulfill those dreams, the temptation to stay there and celebrate can cause us to lose sight of three important truths. First, your life is about much more than accomplishing one all-consuming aspiration; it is about fulfilling God's ultimate purpose for your life, which is to mold you into the image of His Son, Jesus Christ. Yes, accomplishing your dream may play a role in God's purpose for you, but it is not the ultimate goal.

Second, your dreams have been given to you by God and are realized because of God. The process of pursuing, and eventually achieving, your dreams should always result in drawing you closer to the God who gave them to you.

3 (Finally, after you have accomplished one dream, you must remember that God has other dreams for you to pursue. If you and I forget these truths, then our dreams can lead to pride. And God's Word is clear about the danger of pride: "Pride goes before destruction and a haughty spirit before stumbling" (Prov. 16:18).

The Dangers of Pride

Mountaineering tends to attract independent, self-confident people. This is especially true of those who are drawn to big hills. Many climbers create "pride walls" in their homes—places to hang pictures of their summit successes—or create spaces where they can show off their equipment and souvenirs from their travels to the mountains.

There's nothing necessarily wrong with this, of course. Mountain climbers work hard, and they have earned the right to celebrate their successes. In fact, I have a pride wall that highlights some "summits" of my own. On one wall of my office at church, I have framed covers of the more than twenty-six books I've written. Visitors who sit on the couch opposite that wall often look at those covers and comment on them: "Wow, I can't believe how many books you've written! That's quite an accomplishment."

Now, before you judge me too quickly for my wall, I'm willing to bet that you too probably have a wall or shelf in your home or office where you display hard-earned diplomas, certificates, and awards. There is nothing wrong with celebrating summit experiences in our lives. But the downside of such celebrations comes when we begin to allow those achievements to define who we are—when we take more pride in our accomplishments than in serving Christ.

The apostle Paul could have created an impressive wall of accomplishments if he had wanted to. In Philippians 3:5–6, he outlined some of his remarkable religious credentials: "Circumcised the eighth day, of the nation of Israel, of the tribe of Benjamin, a Hebrew of Hebrews; as to the Law, a Pharisee; as to zeal, a persecutor of the church; as to the righteousness which is in the Law, found blameless."

Yet Paul wanted everyone to know that, in comparison to being like Christ, he counted all his accomplishments as "rubbish":

> I count all things to be loss in view of the surpassing value of knowing Christ Jesus my Lord, for whom I have suffered the loss of all things, and count them but rubbish so that I may gain Christ, and may be found in Him, not having a righteousness of my own derived from the Law, but that which is through faith in Christ, the righteousness which comes from God on the basis of faith, that I may know Him and the power of His resurrection and the fellowship of His sufferings, being conformed to His death; in order that I may attain to the resurrection from the dead. (vv. 8–11)

Paul understood that above all the other sins in our lives, God hates pride. What is pride? I think this definition sums it up well; pride is the attitude that credits ourselves with our successes and blames others for our failures. Prideful people think that every good thing in their lives is a result of what they have done. In every conflict, the proud believe

160

that they are right and everyone else is wrong. The proud are convinced they have everything they need and are able to handle any problem.

Why does God hate pride? There is a strong link between pride, ingratitude, and seeking independence from God. We see that illustrated in the first sin ever committed in the universe, recorded in the book of Ezekiel.

Lucifer was an angel who was the head of the highest angelic realm in heaven. He was God's right-hand angel. So what led to Lucifer's downfall? The Bible gives us a glimpse of his sin. God said of Lucifer, "You were blameless in your ways from the day you were created until *unrighteousness* was found in you" (Ezek. 28:15). What was that unrighteousness? Verse 17 tells us: "Your heart was lifted up because of your beauty; you corrupted your wisdom by reason of your splendor."

One day in heaven, Lucifer started thinking, *I'm the real deal. I've got everything anybody could want.* Lucifer made the fatal mistake of forgetting he was a creature and thinking he was the Creator. That pride led him to seek independence from God. We find Lucifer's declaration of independence in Isaiah 14:13–14: "You [Lucifer] said in your heart, 'I will ascend to heaven; I will raise my throne above the stars of God, and I will sit on the mount of assembly in the recesses of the north. I will ascend above the heights of the clouds; I will make myself like the Most High.'" Notice that in these verses, Lucifer focused solely on himself. Over and over again, Lucifer said, "I will . . . I will . . . I will . . . I will . . . I will." He had no thought of God whatsoever.

For that reason, God cast Lucifer out of heaven, and he is now known as Satan, a word that means "adversary." Ever since he was cast out of heaven, Satan has been trying to create a rival shadow empire against God. And the purpose statement of Satan's kingdom is this: "Life apart from God is both possible and preferable. I don't need God. I can live life on my own."

When we understand that pride was the basis of the first sin that led to the satanic rebellion against God, then we can see why God hates pride. Because pride is the original sin, it is the seedbed from which all other sins grow and flourish. C. S. Lewis, who called pride the "great sin," observed, "It is Pride which has been the chief cause of misery in every nation and every family since the world began."[4]

Let's look at three characteristics of pride, so that we can guard against it in our lives.

The Proud Are Lovers of Self

In 2 Timothy 3, the apostle Paul listed various sins that would dominate the last days, and he bookended this list with two main characteristics: "People will be lovers of them-selves . . . rather than lovers of God" (vv. 2, 4 NIV). Now, you may be wondering, "Wait a minute. Doesn't that contradict what Jesus said in Matthew 22:39 about loving our neighbor *as we love ourselves*? Don't we need to love ourselves?" No, there is no contradiction here. The difference between these two verses lies in the fact that Paul was describing the sin of self-love (pride) while Jesus was speaking of healthy self-respect.

Self-respect is treating yourself as you would treat others—as something of value because every person is a creation of God, made in the image of God. Genesis 1:27 tells us,

"God created man in His own image, in the image of God He created him; male and female He created them." Jesus wants us to treat ourselves, and others, with the healthy respect of being God's image-bearers.

The sin of self-love, on the other hand, is treating yourself *better* than you would treat others. It is treating yourself as your own greatest good and highest goal. Like the angel Lucifer, it is the creature pretending to be the Creator; it is Hamlet pretending to be Shakespeare.

Author Peter Kreeft summed it up well: "Humility is thinking less *about* yourself, not thinking less *of* yourself. Pride is arrogance, arrogating to yourself what is really God's."[5]

The Proud Are Consumed with Self

Because the proud place themselves before God, they also place themselves before others.

Proud people have only enough love in their hearts for themselves. They don't care what other people think, do, or feel. The proud are consumed with self, like the character Narcissus. In Greek mythology, when Narcissus saw his reflection in a pool of water, he immediately fell in love with it and spent the rest of his life staring at his own reflection. Is it any wonder Proverbs says, "Pride goes before destruction, and a haughty spirit before stumbling" (16:18)?

Narcissism is what distinguishes pride from vanity. People who are vain at least acknowledge that they need others to feed their vanity. Not so with the proud. They are the center of their own world. A good way to understand the difference between vanity and pride is to think of the difference between movie stars and directors. Movie stars tend to need people to be an adoring audience for them, while directors generally need only power—which leads to the third characteristic of pride.

The Proud Are Driven by Power

At its root, pride is about power. After all, if you don't believe that you answer to God or others, then nothing stands in your way. Our history books—as well as today's headlines—are filled with the devastation caused by prideful people who became so blinded by power that they believed themselves to be above the law.

How ironic that the only One who ever had a right to be proud—Jesus Christ, the Creator of the universe—was the humblest person in human history. Although He had every right to demand that people serve His every whim during His time on earth, He instead said, "The Son of Man did not come to be served, but to serve, and to give His life as a ransom for many" (Matt. 20:28 NIV).

The Humble Are Blessed

Pride is a poison that enters our spiritual bloodstream like venom from the bite of a dangerous snake. The only antidote is humility. In contrast to pride, which causes a person to think, *Everything good in my life is a result of what I have done*, humility is the attitude that realizes, *Everything good in my life is the result of what God or others have done for me*.

There are many biblical passages that teach us about humility, but one that has a unique treasure to enrich our spiritual lives is Matthew 5:3: "Blessed are the poor in spirit, for theirs is the kingdom of heaven." When Jesus preached the Sermon on the Mount, He described what is expected of those who choose to follow Him. A key section of His sermon, known as the Beatitudes, deals with eight specific attitudes that His followers should demonstrate (vv. 3–10).

The Greek word translated "blessed" in this passage means "to be happy" or "overcome with joy." The reason for such joyfulness is because each beatitude is given a reward that will be fulfilled when Jesus Christ returns and establishes His kingdom on the earth. But until that day comes, we who follow Him are to be characterized by these eight attitudes.

The one attitude I want to focus on in this chapter is humility. Let's look at three truths in this verse about humility—the only effective antidote to poisonous pride.

The Humble Recognize Their Spiritual Bankruptcy

When Jesus said, "Blessed are the poor in spirit" (v. 3), He was not referring to material poverty. He was not saying there is something particularly blessed about being financially poor. It doesn't make you less holy or more holy. Instead, He was talking about those who are spiritually impoverished. The late Dallas Willard called them "the spiritual zeros."[6]

Have you ever felt like a "spiritual zero" before? Do you feel as if you are struggling in your Christian life? Do you feel as if you ought to pray more, read the Bible more, and be a better Christian? Jesus was saying, "Be happy. Because one day that struggle you have in your Christian life is going to be satisfied. Yours is going to be the kingdom of God."

People who are humble recognize that they have nothing without God. They know they can't turn to themselves or other people to remove the stain and consequences of their sin, so they turn to God. Andrew Murray, in his classic book *Humility*, put it like this: "True humility comes when before God we see ourselves as nothing, having put aside self, and let God be all."[7]

The humble know that the "sacrifices of God are a broken spirit; a broken and a contrite heart" (Ps. 51:17). In other words, only those who realize they lack the spiritual qualifications to enter God's presence are granted access into God's presence. God gives the humble the keys to His kingdom—as Jesus said, "Theirs is the kingdom of heaven" (Matt. 5:3).

I'm often asked on television or radio talk shows about who is going to populate heaven. "Pastor Jeffress, do you believe [insert Jews, Catholics, Muslims, Mormons, or other religious groups] will be in heaven?" I always answer, "No one goes to heaven or hell in a group. We go one by one, based on our relationship with God. And the only people who are allowed entry into heaven are forgiven people."

Think of it this way. When we humble ourselves, admit our failures to God, and trust in Christ alone, we are given an identification badge marked "Forgiven" that allows us into God's presence—both in this life and in eternity. Without that badge, there is no entrance into God's presence. You can't buy or borrow a badge from someone else. Only God can issue the forgiveness badge.

Early one Sunday morning a number of years ago, when the Super Bowl was being held in Dallas, I was scheduled for a national television interview in front of AT&T Stadium. But I had left my necessary identification for the stadium on my desk at church. So my associate and I stopped by the church to retrieve it. To my chagrin, I discovered that I had also left at home my identification badge that allowed me entry into my office.

The church security guard didn't have a badge that allowed access into my office, nor did my associate. You see, the church had issued me—and me alone—the badge that allowed entry into my office. Desperate and running out of time, I did the only thing I knew to do: I got a hammer and knocked out the glass on the locked door to open it. My associate just stood there dumbstruck, not knowing that destroying a door was an option for a church employee!

However, no one will be able to break into heaven. You have to have the proper identification badge—the one marked "Forgiven"—given to you from the hand of God. As the apostle John wrote, "As many as received Him, to them He gave the right to become children of God, even to those who believe in His name" (John 1:12).

The Humble Reflect the Character of Christ

The humble may be poor in spirit, but that doesn't mean they are spiritually anemic. Instead, they reflect the character of Jesus Christ, who was anything but a weakling.

Throughout His ministry on earth, Jesus demonstrated a remarkable balance between strength and tenderness. In Matthew 11:28–30, He described His character with these words: "Come to Me, all who are weary and heavy-laden, and I will give you rest. Take My yoke upon you and learn from Me, for I am gentle and *humble in heart*, and you will find rest for your souls. For My yoke is easy and My burden light." Jesus was humble, yet He wasn't weak. In John 2:15, He made a whip and drove the corrupt moneychangers out of the temple. He also gave religious hypocrites plenty of tongue lashings. Those aren't the activities of a wimp or sissy.

Think about it: When your world comes crashing down, would you seek shelter in the arms of a weakling? When you need rest, would you go to the cowardly and weak-kneed, who can't protect you? Of course not. When you are weary, you run to someone who, like Jesus, is both powerful and humble.

This reminds me of an insightful observation that appeared years ago in the *Wall Street Journal*: "People want to be lightly governed by strong governments." In an article reflecting on this quote, Joel Belz pointed out, "It's what you've yearned for since you were a small child. You wanted your dad to be big and strong and able to do anything he wanted—except that when he dealt with you, it had to be with tenderness. You wanted that, I think, with every authority figure who was part of your life. . . . Lots of muscle; lots of restraint."[8] That's why, when we need to find rest for our souls, you and I run to the tough tenderness of Jesus Christ.

And if we want to reflect the true character of Christ, we too will develop an attitude of humility.

The Humble Are Dead to Themselves

Nothing is more humbling than dying to yourself. That is why so few are willing to make the sacrifice. But in Matthew 5:3, Jesus said we must humble ourselves if we are to be blessed. In this beatitude, Jesus was saying, "Do you want to really live? If so, the way to live is to die to yourself."

What does it mean to "die to yourself"? Dying to yourself means aligning your personal desires with God's desires. Jesus demonstrated this attitude of self-denial in the garden of Gethsemane when He struggled with going to the cross but prayed, "Not as I will, but as You will" (Matt. 26:39).

Jesus made the same point in different words when He said, "If anyone wants to follow in my footsteps he must give up all right to himself, take up his cross and follow me. For the man who wants to save his life will lose it; but the man who loses his life for my sake will find it. For what good is it for a man to gain the whole world at the price of his own soul? What could a man offer to buy back his soul once he had lost it?" (16:24–26 Phillips). Only when we "lose" our lives by dying to ourselves and following Jesus Christ will we find true, eternal life.

Let's consider a few practical applications of this. What does "dying to yourself" look like in everyday life? Dying to self is listening to the person who is talking to us, without interrupting with our own stories or subconsciously thinking of clever replies. It is swallowing our pride and forgiving a person who has offended us. It is avoiding situations that might tempt us to compromise our witness for Jesus Christ. It is putting down our phones and picking up our Bibles.

Whenever there is a conflict between what we want and what God wants, dying to self means that God wins every time.

Moses: The Humblest Man on Earth

Few men in history had more reasons to be proud than Moses. It would have been easy for Moses to celebrate the many

169

summit experiences in his life. His adoptive mother was the daughter of Pharaoh, the most powerful man in Egypt. As Pharaoh's grandson, Moses grew up in the palace, where he was "educated in all the learning of the Egyptians, and he was a man of power in words and deeds" (Acts 7:22).

Not only did Moses have a privileged upbringing but he also received a supernatural calling. God spoke directly to him at the burning bush. God met with him on Mount Sinai, where He entrusted Moses with His law. And God even permitted Moses to glimpse His glory as He passed by!

Yet what is recorded in the Bible about Moses's character is astounding. Buried in a book that gets very little attention is this amazing statement: "Now the man Moses was *very humble, more than any man who was on the face of the earth*" (Num. 12:3).

Let that sink in.

In God's estimation, Moses was the humblest man alive at the time. What an incredible testimony! Remember, the one characteristic Jesus used to describe Himself was "humble in heart" (Matt. 11:29). God was saying that Moses—more than anyone else alive—was the most like Jesus Christ. That's the kind of accolade Moses could have hung on his pride wall. And a less humble man probably would have. But not Moses.

When you look at Numbers 12:3, you will notice that this verse is set off in parentheses, added almost as an afterthought. Put another way, the statement of Moses's humility is presented humbly. But the implications of this statement might as well be shouted from the mountaintop. Although there are many events in Moses's life that demonstrate his humility, we'll look at only two.

The Elevation of Eldad and Medad

After the Lord miraculously rescued the Israelites from slavery in Egypt, they found themselves surrounded by sand and rocks as far as the eye could see. Soon they began to complain about how much better things had been in Egypt. They said, "We remember the fish which we used to eat free in Egypt, the cucumbers and the melons and the leeks and the onions and the garlic" (Num. 11:5). But in the wilderness, they had nothing to eat but manna. As the leader, Moses received the brunt of their complaints, so he turned and complained to God.

In response to Moses, the Lord told him to gather seventy elders at the tabernacle—the tent that served as the place of worship. There, God would put His Spirit upon these men too, so they could help Moses carry the burden of leadership. When the Holy Spirit came upon the elders, they prophesied by praising God. Then at some point they ceased prophesying, except for two people: Eldad and Medad.

When word got back to Joshua that Eldad and Medad were continuing to prophesy, Joshua was concerned for Moses's reputation and suggested to Moses that he ought to shut these two men up. But Moses said to Joshua, "Would that all the LORD's people were prophets, that the LORD would put His Spirit upon them!" (v. 29).

Moses humbly accepted the fact that God can use anyone He chooses. Moses was more focused on God's message than he was on God's messenger. As long as God's Word was being proclaimed, Moses didn't care who received the praise for proclaiming it.

Moses's attitude reminds me of the apostle Paul, who was imprisoned for preaching the gospel. Word came to

Paul that some of his contemporaries were taking advantage of Paul's imprisonment to make a name for themselves ("If Paul was really anointed by God, do you think God would allow him to languish in prison?"). Yet instead of being embittered about others preaching the gospel for the wrong motive, Paul was energized by it. In his letter to the Philippian Christians, Paul exclaimed, "[They] proclaim Christ out of selfish ambition rather than from pure motives, thinking to cause me distress in my imprisonment. What then? Only that in every way, whether in pretense or in truth, Christ is proclaimed; and in this I rejoice. Yes, and I will rejoice" (Phil. 1:17–18).

The Murmuring of Miriam

It can be tough on older siblings when their little brother or sister becomes the leader of the family. Petty jealousies often ensue. That was certainly the case with Moses's older siblings, Miriam and Aaron.

After Moses refused to silence the voice of God spoken through Eldad and Medad, Miriam and Aaron leveled a complaint against their younger brother. Numbers 12:1–2 says, "Miriam and Aaron spoke against Moses . . . and they said, 'Has the LORD indeed spoken only through Moses? Has He not spoken through us as well?'"

Miriam and Aaron were likely jealous of Moses. Who knows, there may have been years of sibling rivalry between them and their younger brother. You could almost hear Miriam think to herself, *Who does Moses think he is? If it wasn't for me placing him in that basket when he was an infant and watching it drift on the Nile, Pharaoh's daughter would have never found him. He would have died like all those other infant boys.*

They may also have felt slighted because God's Spirit had been poured out on the seventy elders but not on them. "After all," Miriam and Aaron may have said to each other, "We are followers of God. We ought to have an equal voice. Moses isn't that great. We're just as important as he is."

Whatever the motive may have been, Miriam and Aaron lashed out against Moses. But when the Lord heard their complaint, He was unhappy. Calling Aaron and Miriam forward, He informed them that He alone was able to choose with whom He would communicate. Though the Lord was angry with both Miriam and Aaron, because Miriam was the leading voice of criticism, God punished her with leprosy.

If Miriam had been my sister, I would have said to her, in as humble a way as I could muster, "Serves you right. That's what you get for speaking against the Lord's anointed."

But that's not how Moses reacted.

Aaron asked his younger brother to intercede with God on Miriam's behalf. In response, Moses offered a simple, direct prayer: "O God, heal her, I pray!" (v. 13). The Lord did heal Miriam, though she had to suffer the consequence of being out of fellowship with the community for seven days.

As many of us know all too well, the wounds of family and friends can cut deeper than the attacks of enemies. But regardless of who is criticizing us, those who have developed humility will hold their tongue and allow God to defend them—as Moses did.

173

How to Develop Humility

My predecessor at my church, the legendary Dr. W. A. Criswell, used to keep a beautifully bound book on the coffee table in his office. Visitors were intrigued by the title embossed in gold leaf: *My Humility . . . And How I Achieved It.* When they opened the book, they discovered that it was filled with 150 blank pages! I think of that "book" whenever I attempt to suggest how to develop humility. Anyone who thinks he or she has arrived hasn't! Nevertheless, Scripture does offer some practical insights on how to develop humility—a character quality that is essential for our spiritual survival in a hostile world.

Accept the Fact That You Aren't Indispensable

Like Moses, I also have a brother and sister (though younger). They certainly aren't like Miriam and Aaron, but the truth is we did occasionally tattle on one another—especially when one of us was feeling jealous of the other. And in Numbers 11, we see the same thing happening with the children of Israel. A tattletale came to Moses saying, "Eldad and Medad are prophesying in the camp" (v. 27). He was saying, "Moses, a couple of guys are doing *your* job! Who do they think they are? You should put a stop to it!"

But Moses was broad-shouldered enough to realize that God could use others in leading the people. Moses had nothing to lose, so he had nothing to prove.

Moses's attitude reflected his humility. *If God wants to use other members of the community to accomplish His purpose, then that's His business.* If we are honest, many of us struggle with that attitude. It's easy to feel as if we are indispensable. Entrepreneurs who start companies often find it difficult to step down even when it becomes apparent that new leadership is necessary. The same is true for pastors who start churches or who have served in churches for decades. The simple truth is, none of us is indispensable.

If you want to see how indispensable you are, I have a three-step experiment you ought to try. First, fill a bucket with water. Next, place your arm in the bucket all the way to your elbow. Finally, quickly remove your arm from the bucket. The size of the "hole" you leave in the water is a precise measurement of the "hole" you will leave in the world when you're no longer around. That's a good reminder whenever you and I are tempted to wonder how the world could get along without us!

No matter what measure of success God allows us to experience in this life, we should make it a practice never to read or believe our own press clippings. We must be careful not to celebrate our summits too often or too long. Otherwise, we will be tempted to think that we arrived at the top all by ourselves. We didn't.

Humility is the realization that every good thing in our lives is ultimately the result of what God and/or others have done for us. In 1 Corinthians 4:7, Paul asks a penetrating question: "What do you have that you did not receive? And if you did receive it, why do you boast as if you had not received it?" The truth is, everything we are tempted to feel prideful about—our vocational achievements, our wealth, or even our good looks—ultimately can be traced to other people who helped us or to God.

175

Instead of lingering on the summit in a self-congratulatory celebration, why not send a thank-you note to a person who has contributed to your success or a thank-you prayer to the God who made it all possible?

Cultivate the Habit of Silence

When Miriam and Aaron spoke against their brother, Moses did not immediately defend himself. Numbers 12 includes no record of Moses criticizing his siblings or putting them in their place. ("If you're so great, why didn't you have a bigger part in *The Ten Commandments* movie?") Instead, Moses humbly trusted God to deal with his irritating siblings.

The proud can't control their passions, so they quickly strike back against those who speak ill against them. They are like seasoned cop Jim Malone in the film *The Untouchables*, who famously explained what he called "the Chicago Way": "He pulls a knife; you pull a gun. He sends one of yours to the hospital; you send one of his to the morgue."[9]

But that's not the way it should be with the people of God. Moses's experience reminds us that God is more than capable of defending us. We don't have to run our own defense by running our mouths; God can and will do it so much better. Jesus, who endured the greatest injustice of all, provides us with an illustration of that truth by His example on the cross: "And while being reviled, He did not revile in return; while suffering, he uttered no threats, but kept entrusting Himself to Him who judges righteously" (1 Pet. 2:23).

Pray for Those Who Hurt You

It is interesting to note that though Moses did not speak to others after being slandered by Miriam, he did speak to God about Miriam—offering a prayer on her behalf.

The proud often have a hard time praying, especially praying for those whom they consider enemies. Why? In general, prayer is an admission that we have a need that we cannot meet—whether that need is for forgiveness, material provisions, deliverance from difficulty, or justice after being hurt by others. But when it comes to praying for our enemies, prayer requires us to put their interests above our own desires—like the desire to see our adversaries boil in oil for eternity! Yet when we pray for those who have wronged us, as Moses did, we demonstrate the same humility Jesus showed on the cross toward those who crucified Him: "Father, forgive them; for they do not know what they are doing" (Luke 23:34).

Veteran mountaineer David Breashears said, "Getting to the summit is the easy part; it's getting back down that's hard."[10] This is not only true in the life of a mountain climber; it's also true in the life of a Christian. Pride is easy; humility is hard.

But if we are going to make it to the summit in spite of the headwinds and obstacles that constantly assail us, we must empty our backpack of pride. Pride not only weighs us down but also deprives us of receiving the help we need from God and others to reach the summit. If you really wish God to lift you up and help you attain what is best for your life, then you must put down your pride and pick up humility. As the apostle James reminded us, "Humble yourselves in the presence of the Lord, and He will exalt you" (James 4:10).

Learn from the Past

Juliane Koepcke didn't grow up like most girls. Her parents were well-known German zoologists who worked and lived in the Peruvian rain forest. When she was fourteen years old, Juliane's parents established a research station in the heart of a rain forest, and she became a "jungle child."[1]

Life in the forest was difficult. They had no running water or electricity. Every morning, they shook out their rubber boots to dislodge the poisonous spiders that had taken up residence in them overnight. Her days consisted of home-schooling lessons in math and language, as well as research excursions into the jungle to study insects, birds, fish, other wildlife, and plants.

However, the educational authorities in Peru didn't approve of her schooling. So, after eighteen months of traipsing through the rain forest, Juliane traveled to Lima to finish high school, which she did in December 1971. Her mother flew to Lima to retrieve Juliane for the Christmas holiday, but since there was a graduation dance on December 22 and a graduation ceremony the following day, they decided to fly back to their jungle home on Christmas Eve.

Every flight was fully booked, except for one airplane belonging to Lansa, the smallest airline—with the worst safety record—in Peru. On board, Juliane and her mother sat two rows from the back. She took the window seat, her mother sat in the middle, and a heavyset man was on the aisle. "I think it will be okay," her mother said.

Those words would haunt Juliane for decades.

Only fifteen minutes from reaching their destination, the plane flew into a thundercloud. Turbulence rocked the plane this way and that. Christmas presents, jackets, and suitcases that had been stored in the overhead compartments flew around the plane's cabin. Glancing out the window, Juliane saw a blinding light over the right wing, and then they began to plummet.

The noise in the plane was deafening. People were screaming, and the engines roared. And then, as if someone had flipped a switch, all was quiet. Juliane, still strapped to her seat, was outside the plane. Her mother was gone.

Falling headfirst from nearly ten thousand feet, Juliane saw the canopy of the forest spinning and coming closer. The treetops looked like broccoli, she later recalled. Somewhere on the descent she blacked out, lost her glasses, and the capillaries in her eyes burst, causing them to appear blood red. Her seat somehow righted itself before she hit the trees, because once on the ground, she was relatively unharmed, with only a concussion, a broken collarbone, and a gash on her left calf.

When Juliane came to, she was by herself. She didn't see any wreckage around her. She knew it would be impossible for rescuers to find her under the thick canopy of trees, so she would have to rescue herself. Thankfully, she knew the jungle and was comfortable in it. She attuned her ears to the forest and heard the trickling sound of a stream. She knew that streams led to creeks, creeks led to rivers, and people lived along rivers. So she moved toward the sound of the trickling water.

She intended to follow along the banks of the stream, but the jungle was such a tangle of trees and vines that it was almost impassable. She could walk along the shallows, but she knew stingrays buried themselves in the soft mud along the banks and that piranhas are dangerous only in low water. So she decided to wade into the middle of the stream and float. She would have to watch out for the alligator-like reptiles called caimans, but she knew they generally didn't attack people.

During the day, Juliane kept to the stream. At night, she came ashore and, as best she could, warded off the biting insects that tangled in her hair and tried to burrow into her nose and ears—all the time shivering from the ice-cold rain. All she had to eat was a bag of Christmas candy she'd found, which would last only a few days. Everything else, she knew, could be poisonous. But she also knew that she could drink from the middle of the stream with little danger of dysentery because the area was uninhabited.

She floated for days until she recognized the call of hoatzins, large birds that nest along sizable rivers and open water. Following the birdcall, Juliane walked into a spacious clearing next to a river. There, she saw a boat beside a well-worn trail that led to a shelter. The shelter was empty, but the next day she heard voices. Three men emerged from the forest and were frightened at her presence, thinking she was a river spirit, which were said to have fair skin and blonde hair. Her bloodshot eyes didn't help ease their minds. But she said in Spanish, "I'm a girl who was in the Lansa crash. My name is Juliane."[2]

Learn from the Past

Ninety-one people, including Juliane's mother, perished in the crash of Lansa Flight 508. Juliane was the sole survivor, enduring eleven days in an Amazonian rain forest. Her story is remarkable not only because she miraculously lived after being ejected from the plane but because she was able to trek through the jungle with multiple injuries in only a sundress and one sandal.

Whether you are climbing a mountain, picking your way through a dangerous rain forest, or navigating through some other challenging situation, survival often hinges not so much on doing everything exactly right but on not compounding mistakes by making additional ones. And one of the best ways to mitigate missteps is learning from the experiences and examples of the past.

During her ordeal in the Peruvian rain forest, Juliane relied on her past experience of living in the jungle and the things she had learned from her parents. Her father had taught her that streams led to rivers and rivers led to people. He also had taught her that stingrays and piranhas thrive in shallow water and that caimans are virtually harmless to humans. Her mother, an ornithologist, taught her the habits of jungle birds and their birdcalls, including the call of the hoatzin.

Juliane's ability to remember and apply the lessons she had learned saved her life.

As a general rule, adventurers who survive treacherous undertakings—whether climbing Mount Everest or exploring an icy continent—are those who learn from the past. They consult with experts, study others who attempted the feat before them, and gain insight from their examples about how to cope with life-threatening situations. Even ordinary men and women who do not choose a life of adventure but are unexpectedly thrust into danger—as Juliane was—have a significantly better chance of surviving if they are able to remember and apply what they have learned in the past.

As we've seen throughout this book, what is true for survivalists in critical situations is equally true for Christians who are committed to living godly lives in this world. As believers in Jesus Christ, we must be diligent to develop the survival skill of learning from the past. Our ability to apply what we have learned and to avoid others' mistakes—or our own past mistakes—can make all the difference in thriving with our faith intact.

The Value of History

These days, we are so focused on the future that we have largely forgotten the importance of history. Who has time to learn about people who lived hundreds of years ago when we are busy trying to keep up with the next new fashion trend, technological innovation, or social media challenge? "History is more or less bunk," industrialist Henry Ford famously said. "We want to live in the present, and the only history that is worth [anything] is the history we make today."[3]

Our society seems to agree with Ford. As showcased in the popular "Man on the Street" interviews on late-night comedy shows, historical illiteracy among the general population has reached new highs. According to a recent survey, most residents of the United States are "alarmingly ignorant of America's history and heritage."[4] Only one in three Americans can pass the US citizenship exam, and that number plummets to a dismal 19 percent of those under age forty-five. More than half of those surveyed didn't even know which countries the United States fought in World War II!

Lest you think this lack of historical knowledge is strictly an American problem, consider that one-fifth of British teenagers today think that Winston Churchill was a fictional character, while more than 50 percent believe that Sherlock Holmes, Robin Hood, and King Arthur were real.[5] With such a limited understanding of history, is it any wonder that so many people today have no perspective about the world in which we live?

Someone who doesn't think history is bunk is the Author of history. After all, history is ultimately "His story." God wants us to learn the lessons of those who came before us. In fact, "remember" is the theme of an entire book in the Bible.

No fewer than sixteen times in the book of Deuteronomy, God instructed His people to "remember" their history. Deuteronomy is a collection of Moses's final words to the Israelites before they entered the promised land. For forty years, the people had wandered in the wilderness until the unbelieving, disobedient generation had died (Num. 14:29–32; 32:11–13). Finally, the new generation was old enough to inherit the land that God had promised to them.

The word *Deuteronomy* comes from two Hebrew words: *deuteros* means "second," and *nomos* means "law." In other words, this book is a second giving of the law—a recap for the next generation. In this book, Moses gave a comprehensive review of God's commands and Israel's experience in hopes that the next generation would not repeat the mistakes of their parents.

When Deuteronomy was written, Moses was advanced in years. He understood that he would not be the one to lead the Israelites into the promised land; he had forfeited that opportunity because of his own sin. But he wanted the Israelites to be successful under their new leader, Joshua. So he stood before them one last time and urged them to do something that would guarantee their success in the new land: remember what God had done in the past.

Moses reminded the Israelites of important truths the previous generation had learned and then presented them with a simple choice.

> See, I am setting before you today a blessing and a curse: the blessing, if you listen to the commandments of the LORD your God, which I am commanding you today; and the curse, if you do not listen to the commandments of the LORD your God, but turn aside from the way which I am commanding you today, by following other gods which you have not known. (Deut. 11:26–28)

The older generation had essential lessons to teach the young Israelites about the consequences of idolatry and the blessings of obedience. But was the next generation willing to learn?

The same question applies to you and me today. Throughout the sixty-six books that make up our Bible, we have stories of heroes who teach us the value of faith, sacrifice, love, and hope. We also have examples that show us the consequences of failures, betrayal, lying, and immorality. If we are willing to learn from it, the history we find within the pages of Scripture provides truth and wisdom—and it challenges us to be more like Christ. As Paul said in Romans 15:4, "Whatever was written in earlier times was written for our instruction." The study of history as recorded in the Scriptures, Paul said, is a source of "perseverance . . . encouragement . . . [and] hope" (v. 4).

If you and I are going to thrive spiritually in a world that has abandoned biblical values, we cannot disregard what thousands of years of history teach us. Instead, we should put into practice Job 8:8–9: "Inquire of past generations, and consider the things searched out by their fathers. For we are only of yesterday and know nothing, because our days on earth are as a shadow."

In this chapter, that is just what we are going to do.

Heeding the Warnings of History

Philosopher George Santayana famously said, "Those who cannot remember the past are condemned to repeat it."[6] This is a message we see not only throughout the Old Testament but in the New Testament as well. For example, when the apostle Paul wrote to the wayward church in Corinth, he used the example of the ancient Israelites to demonstrate the consequences of falling into sinful habits. He wrote, "These things happened to them [the Israelites] as an example, and they were written for our instruction, upon whom the ends of the ages have come" (1 Cor. 10:11). It's as if Paul were saying, "Pay particular attention to the history I'm about to tell you, so you can avoid making the same mistakes—and suffering the same consequences—as the Israelites."

As Moses did in Deuteronomy, the apostle Paul began his teaching in 1 Corinthians with the history of Israel's relationship with the Lord. Then he applied the early Hebrews' history to the current situation in Corinth. Finally, Paul issued his readers a word of warning. Though the Israelites had enjoyed fellowship with God and had been sustained by Christ, Paul said, "With most of them God was not well-pleased" (10:5).

Why wasn't God pleased with the ancient Israelites? They worshiped idols, engaged in sexual immorality, and grumbled against the Lord and His spokesperson. In 1 Corinthians 10:6, Paul explained, "These things happened as examples for us." Then in verse 11, he restated the conclusion: "These things happened to them as an example, and they were written for our instruction, upon whom the ends of the ages have come."

The Greek word for "example" is *typos*, from which we get our English word *type*. This word originally meant "the mark from a blow"—an impression. I'm going to date myself, but I'm old enough to remember writing term papers for school on a *type*writer. Typewriters had metal type bars—or a type wheel, if you were really fancy—that carried the letters of the alphabet. When you pressed a key, say the letter *R*, a leveler in the typewriter moved the type bar, striking an ink ribbon against a piece of paper. What was left on the paper was an impression—a distinctive mark—of, in this case, the letter *R*. Similarly, the history of Israel was recorded in the Bible to make a lasting impression on us.

Notice also that Paul said, "These things *happened*." Paul wasn't teaching a lesson from a fairy tale, myth, or legend. Paul stressed that this was the factual record of real events that happened to real people in a real place and time. God works in and through history, in the lives of flesh-and-blood people. And in this case, the history of the ancient Hebrews was "written for our instruction," for those of us who live in the present last days—or as Paul put it, "upon whom the ends of the ages have come" (1 Cor. 10:11). Paul provided a history lesson to help us reason theologically, so we can reach the same conclusions about life as God does.

Paul concluded, "Therefore let him who thinks he stands take heed that he does not fall" (v. 12). Let's learn from the experiences and warnings of history so that we are not doomed to repeat it.

Josiah: The King Who Allowed History to Shape His Future

An instructive example of somebody who learned from the past was the Old Testament king Josiah. Given his family's background, young Josiah had every reason to become an evil king, but he didn't. In fact, he was one of the most righteous kings in the history of Judah.

We are first introduced to Josiah at his coronation—when he was only eight years old! "Josiah was eight years old when he became king, and he reigned thirty-one years in Jerusalem. He did right in the sight of the LORD, and walked in the ways of his [forefather] David and did not turn aside to the right or to the left" (2 Chron. 34:1–2).

If anyone ever had to survive in a pagan culture, it was young King Josiah. For the previous fifty-seven years, the nation had openly defied God and His law. Josiah's grandfather, Manasseh, had committed some of the evilest acts ever recorded in Judah's history. King Manasseh had led the people into idolatry; practiced human sacrifice; worshiped the sun, moon, and stars; and consulted with sorcerers and witches. According to 2 Chronicles 33:9, "Manasseh misled Judah and the inhabitants of Jerusalem to do more evil than the nations whom the LORD destroyed before the sons of Israel."

It's almost impossible to imagine, but when Manasseh's son Amon took over the throne, he somehow multiplied his father's evil and stole the title of "Judah's Worst King." In fact, Amon's rule was so vile that it lasted only two years. At the early age of twenty-four, King Amon was assassinated in the palace in Jerusalem—a murder that may have been witnessed by his son Josiah.

Young Josiah courageously rejected the pattern of his grandfather and father. He refused to accept that he was a helpless victim of a "generational curse." Instead, he decided to follow in the footsteps of his hero, King David, and refused to turn away from the Lord, either "to the right or to the left" (34:2).

Learning the Lessons of History

When Josiah came to the throne at the tender age of eight, court officials served as his mentors. But the real influence on the young king was his mother. What seems like an offhand comment in 2 Kings 22:1—"his mother's name was

Jedidah"—hints at something more significant. Josiah's mother was named in Scripture because, as the queen mother, she was highly respected and exerted tremendous influence on her son's spiritual, educational, and political development.

Along with the court officials, Jedidah was instrumental in ensuring that Josiah would do "right in the sight of the LORD" (2 Chron. 34:2). Although her husband, Amon, was a horrible example for Josiah, Jedidah refused to allow their son to become a casualty of Amon's spiritual delinquency. She was determined to pour into her son a love for and fear of God.

Jedidah is a tremendous example for mothers married to unbelieving husbands or single mothers who are determined to rear godly children. She understood that the most important thing we can do during the few short years we have with our children is to teach them how to follow God. If you are a parent, your most important task is not to raise your kids' SAT scores, get them into a good college, or develop them into star athletes. Your most important job as a parent is to teach your children what it means to love, follow, and obey Jesus Christ.

For eight years, Josiah sat under the teaching of his mother and the court officials, absorbing the lessons of history, of what God expected from him, and how a king should rule God's people. Then, when he was sixteen, Josiah personally "began to seek the God of his father David" (v. 3).

Although Josiah's mother was faithful to teach him about God, there came a time when Josiah had to decide to follow God for himself. Teenagers and young adults, you are responsible for growing in your knowledge of God. While your parents and church leaders can provide insight that helps you understand Scripture, only you can strengthen your mind with the Word of God; nobody else can do that for you. If you want to stand firm in your faith and have a godly life that honors the Lord, it begins with you.

Applying the Lessons of History

Josiah grew in his faith, and the Lord began stirring the king's heart. By the time Josiah turned twenty, the lessons he had learned from his mother and the court officials, and the direction he was receiving from the Lord, came into sharp focus. He realized that his beliefs and his nation's godly history were in direct conflict with the religious practices of the citizens in his kingdom.

Josiah understood that the first and greatest commandment was "You shall have no other gods before Me" (Exod. 20:3). As the Israelites prepared to enter the promised land, which was filled with people who worshiped pagan deities, God commanded them to "put away the foreign gods which are in your midst" (Josh. 24:23). In fact, they were told not even to mention the names of these other gods. Tragically, Israel ignored God's commands and incurred His harsh judgment for tolerating the worship of other deities.

So Josiah took decisive action to remove idolatry from the land. "He began to purge Judah and Jerusalem of the high places, the Asherim, the carved images and the molten images" (2 Chron. 34:3). He tore down the altars to pagan gods and beat the images of idols into powder to prevent them from being used for false worship.

Our country could learn an important lesson from Josiah. Today, many people in America believe that all religious systems are equally valid. But what we celebrate as diversity, God condemns as idolatry. Although our constitution grants every citizen the right to worship or not worship any god he or she chooses, that right in no way changes God's attitude toward idolatry. The First Amendment does not usurp the first commandment. The Bible is clear: any nation that chooses to renounce the true God in order to embrace and elevate other gods will face God's judgment.

Back to the Book

At age twenty-six, after he cleansed the land of idols, King Josiah ordered the temple in Jerusalem to be repaired. Money was collected, workers were hired, and the project was begun.

In the process of carrying out the work, the high priest discovered a treasure that had been lost. The Bible says, "When they were bringing out the money which had been brought into the house of the LORD, Hilkiah the priest found the book of the law of the LORD given by Moses. Hilkiah responded and said to Shaphan the scribe, 'I have found the book of the law in the house of the LORD'" (vv. 14–15). For the first time in more than half a century, God's scroll was unrolled and read.

Josiah's response to hearing the Word of God read to him was grief, which he demonstrated by tearing his robe. Although these scrolls had been gathering dust for decades, God's Word had lost none of its power. As soon as Josiah heard the book of the law, he was convicted of the way he and his nation had fallen short of God's standard.

The writer of Hebrews reminds us, "The word of God is living and active and sharper than any two-edged sword, and piercing as far as the division of soul and spirit, of both joints and marrow, and able to judge the thoughts and intentions of the heart" (4:12). As I once heard another pastor put it, "God's Word is always doing something to those who read or hear it!"

Is there a Bible gathering dust somewhere in your home? Open it up, remove the cobwebs from its pages if necessary, and let God speak to you. As Martin Luther wisely said, "The Bible is alive, it speaks to me; it has feet, it runs after me; it has hands, it lays hold of me."[7]

God's Word certainly did something to Josiah. Hearing it reminded the king of how far the nation had drifted from God. But Josiah did not simply wallow in his grief over sin. Instead, his grief led to repentance. The word *repentance* means "change of mind." Repentance is a change of mind that leads to a change in direction in life. True repentance always results in action.

It certainly did for Josiah. As he was reminded of the truths from God's Word that he had learned from his mother, the king gathered the people before the temple and publicly read the "words of the book of the covenant which was found in the house of the LORD" (2 Chron. 34:30). Josiah committed himself to fulfilling the Lord's covenant, and so did the people. For the rest of Josiah's reign, the people "did not turn from following the LORD God of their fathers" (v. 33).

Josiah had learned and applied the lessons of history well, and he and his people reaped the benefits.

Learning and Applying the Lessons of History

Because of our human nature, unless we make conscious changes, our future will often look very similar to our past.

This is why Solomon wrote, "There is nothing new under the sun" (Eccles. 1:9).

Since the beginning of human history, we have been following in the footsteps of our first ancestors, Adam and Eve. We have wanted to be like God; we have blamed others, including God, for our own faults; and we have tried, in vain, to cover our sins. Technology may have advanced, but human nature hasn't. Is it any wonder why the present looks very much like the past? We still fight wars. People are still murdered. Families still become estranged. Lies are still told. Sins of every kind still run rampant through the human heart.

Unless we learn and apply the lessons of history, our future will be no different from our past. So what do we do? We should take history seriously, learn from our own past experiences, and find heroes to emulate.

Take History Seriously

When I took history classes in junior high and high school, the coursework involved memorizing a lot of dates, names, and places. I have to admit that, back then, I thought history was boring! Considering how many dull facts and details we had to memorize during our school years, no wonder so many adults find the study of history to be a waste of time.

But history is more than dates and names and places on a map. History is a record of the hatreds and loves, the fears and desires, the victories and defeats of human beings. History is human. And because humans are made in the image of God, we should take history seriously—as God does.

I have learned to appreciate and learn from books, television shows, and films about significant people and events in history, in addition to the ones recorded in Scripture. For example, right now I'm reading *Leadership: In Turbulent Times* by Doris Kearns Goodwin, which details how Abraham Lincoln, Theodore Roosevelt, Franklin Roosevelt, and Lyndon B. Johnson dealt with crises during their presidencies.[8] A book like this is certainly no substitute for the Bible, which I read every day, but it illustrates universal principles about success and failure. All truth is ultimately God's truth, and there is a lot of truth we can learn from studying the past.

Another way you can learn from the past is to take your own family history seriously. Perhaps you've noticed that how you relate to your spouse or how you discipline your children mimics your mother or father. I sometimes find myself using the same phrases with Amy or my daughters that my father used when speaking with my mother or with me. Sometimes it's funny—other times it's scary!

The habits you learned from your family can be positive or negative. If they are positive, keep doing them. If negative, make a change. If, for example, your father disciplined you by yelling and belittling you, and you find yourself falling into the same pattern while disciplining your children, then make the necessary changes to your parenting style. Understand where it comes from and commit to doing things differently.

On the other hand, if there is something in your family history that is positive, then pass along those traditions to your children. One young mother in my church told me that her parents had a tradition of serving meals at a homeless shelter every Thanksgiving Day, as a way of expressing gratitude and serving the Lord and others. When she had children of her own, she was eager to continue that tradition in her own family.

You can also learn from your family history when it comes to your health and well-being. Both my parents died at a relatively early age. After their passing, I resolved, as much as it was possible for me to control, to take extra care of my health. So every day, I eat a bowl of bran flakes, maintain a healthy diet, and engage in some kind of physical exercise. I don't do these things because I want to; I do them because I have learned from my family's history. I have now lived longer than both of my parents did. The Lord has been gracious to me. But I also took my family's medical history seriously and determined that, God willing, I would break the cycle of early death.

Your family history can also be a key to potential pitfalls in your spiritual life. If immorality is a part of your family heritage, don't be surprised if you are tempted in that area as well. If addictions are common in your family, you need to be on guard against that possibility in your life. In my own family—going generations back—there has been an unhealthy focus on money that I've had to work to avoid. As King Josiah looked at his father's and grandfather's idolatry and immorality, he was determined not to make the same mistakes.

We can learn good things from our family history as well. I remember as a little boy attending a funeral service with my grandfather for an African-American man who worked for him. The man had gotten drunk one night and became embroiled in a fight in which he was stabbed to death. I think my grandfather and I were the only white faces at the funeral, which, at that time, was held in a section of the cemetery reserved for minorities. The pastor lambasted the departed man for his drunkenness, insinuating not so subtly that he got what he deserved.

As the minister was about to conclude in prayer, my grandfather stood up and interrupted the service. He said, "Pastor, before you conclude, I have a few words I would like to say about my friend." And for the next moments, my grandfather extolled the virtues of the man who had been his friend and employee for so many years. After the service, the man's family and friends surrounded my grandfather, thanking him for his willingness to stand up and set the record straight. I learned from my grandfather that day what real courage looked like.

Learn from Your Past

We can certainly learn how to survive in challenging times from the experiences of others. But we can also learn from our own history as well.

Let's face it: we all make mistakes. Though our missteps come in a variety of shapes and sizes, most of us have at least one major blunder in our past. Perhaps you made a poor financial decision that proved to be disastrous for your financial security. Or maybe you were presented with a great opportunity, but you procrastinated due to laziness or fear and ended up missing out on something that would have been emotionally, physically, or financially rewarding. Or possibly your mistake was more life-changing, such as an innocent friendship that turned into an immoral affair or a decision that destroyed your reputation.

As you consider your past mistakes, you might be wondering, *Can God ever forgive me? Even if God does forgive me, will I have to spend the rest of my life suffering the consequences for my mistake? If God is really in control of everything, did His plan for my life include this tremendous mistake?* And most importantly, *Can I ever hope to recover from my mistake?*

The answer is yes. I can think of many missteps I've made in my life, including one in particular (and trust me, you'll never guess what it was, so you can quit trying!). As much as I regret that mistake, it had a very positive effect on my life. First, that failure has, in a way, inoculated me against ever making that blunder again. Anytime I even come close to a similar situation, I run in the opposite direction. Second, I've had the opportunity on many occasions to warn others about making a similar mistake in their lives.

When I reflect on my mistake—and the resulting consequences—I think about King David's testimony about his sin with Bathsheba and the steep price he paid for that sin. Although his failure was moral and mine was not, I can still identify with his words: "Before I was afflicted I went astray, but now I keep Your word" (Ps. 119:67). Reflecting on his past mistake and the resulting, painful consequences of that failure motivated David to walk more closely with his God in the future.

Maybe your past isn't riddled with colossal failures but a more gradual turning away from spiritual things. Perhaps some of you, as a child or a young adult, made the decision to trust in Christ. You received the forgiveness of your sins. But since that time, you've strayed from God. Your spiritual life has slowly eroded, and things happened after you became

a Christian that you're not proud of. Now yo
ing, *What is God's attitude toward me, a Christ.
wandered away from Him? Can I be forgiven?*

Unfortunately, life has no rewind button. But
says that no matter what has happened in your ,   .io
matter what mistake you made or how far you've wandered
from Him, God can still shape you to become more like Jesus
Christ. Although we don't want to get stuck in our past, we
can certainly learn from it.

Think of the apostle Peter. Matthew 26:69–75 records
that on the night Jesus was arrested, Peter strayed from his
faith and failed miserably. But Jesus wasn't willing to allow
Peter's failure to be the final word in his life. Instead, He offered forgiveness and restoration to His friend. Three days
later, when Jesus was raised from the dead, the first apostle
He appeared to was Peter. Think about it: He could have
chosen His beloved disciple, John, the one who was faithful
and stood with Him until the end. Instead, He chose Peter,
the one who denied Him. This was Jesus's way of saying,
"I forgive you."

A mere six weeks later, the same Peter who had disappointed the Lord earlier was standing before thousands on
the southern steps of the temple in Jerusalem, courageously
preaching about the resurrection of Jesus Christ—and thousands of people that day came to faith in Christ. Recently,
I preached on those very steps in Jerusalem where Peter
preached perhaps the most powerful sermon in history and
was reminded by Peter's story that no matter what mistakes
we have made, our failure doesn't have to be the last chapter
in our life story. God is not only willing to forgive us but is
also willing to use us again.

Find Heroes to Emulate

I know this may sound childish to mature, sophisticated adults, but we all need to find and emulate heroes. As Thomas Carlyle said, "No sadder proof can be given by a man of his own littleness than disbelief in great men."[9] All great men and women had heroes. Alexander the Great admired the heroes in Homer's *Iliad* and *Odyssey*. Julius Caesar was motivated by Alexander the Great. Abraham Lincoln was inspired by George Washington.

When it comes to living out our faith in an increasingly secular culture, we have countless Christian heroes to learn from and emulate. For example, Hudson Taylor spent more than fifty years serving in China as a missionary. During his time there, he established the China Inland Mission and personally influenced hundreds of people to become missionaries. Even today, many missionaries still say they became interested in mission work after reading biographies of Taylor.[10]

One missionary who was inspired by Taylor was Amy Carmichael. Born into a wealthy family in Ireland, Amy decided to become a missionary after she heard Taylor speak about the need for missions. In many ways, she patterned her missionary work after Taylor's. She too founded a mission and opened an orphanage without fund-raising but instead through asking the Lord to provide what was needed. For fifty-six years, she rescued hundreds of children from physical and sexual abuse in India, becoming known as "Amma," or mother, to them.[11]

Amy Carmichael learned from the example of her hero and emulated much of his ministry as she fulfilled her own unique calling from God. Isn't this something along the lines of what Paul was getting at when he wrote in 1 Corinthians 11:1, "Be imitators of me, just as I also am of Christ," or in Philippians 4:9, "The things you have learned and received and heard and seen in me, practice these things, and the God of peace will be with you"?

I've written extensively about my heroes in other books. They include my father and mother, who modeled for me what a Christlike life looks like. I also have learned from the late W. A. Criswell and Howard G. Hendricks, both of whom served as my mentors and friends. And there are many others, inside and outside of ministry, whom I admire and emulate.

Who are your heroes? Heroes give us courage. They remind us that others too have faced daunting challenges and have overcome them with dignity and grace. The issues you face are not unique; others have gone through similar challenges. Learn from them. Derive courage from their example. When you discover and apply the lessons of the past, you too can do more than merely survive in these present last days—you can thrive!

Help Others

At the end of Steven Spielberg's movie *Schindler's List*, Nazi Oskar Schindler (played by Liam Neeson) is about to flee from the advancing Russian army. Surrounded by more than one thousand Jews whom Schindler had saved from Hitler's gas chambers, Itzhak Stern (portrayed by Ben Kingsley) hands Schindler a gold ring and says, "Whoever saves one life saves the world entire."[1]

I remembered this Jewish saying after stumbling on a story that came out of the tragedy of September 11, 2001. Many tales have been told about that horrific day—you might even have one of your own. But the story of Brian Clark and Stanley Praimnath captured my attention. Both men worked in the South Tower of 2 World Trade Center in New York. Brian was a vice president at Euro Brokers on the eighty-fourth floor, and Stanley was an executive for Fuji Bank on the eighty-first floor.

Brian was a volunteer fire marshal, so he sprang into action when he saw the explosion in the North Tower. He grabbed his reflector vest, flashlight, and whistle and began to gather those on the floor for evacuation. Everyone's attention was focused on what was happening in the neighboring tower . . . until a sudden explosion in the South Tower caused the building to sway. Brian didn't know exactly what was happening, but he knew one thing for sure: they needed to get out of the building immediately.

With eight others, Brian descended Stairway C. When they made it down to the eighty-first floor, they encountered debris and a woman making her way *up* the stairwell. She said that the stairway was obstructed and that flames were below the eighty-first floor. The only way of escape, she insisted, was the roof. She was confident that helicopters would rescue them there. As she continued up the stairs, the group Brian was leading down began debating what to do. Just then, Brian heard someone crying for help. It was Stanley.

Stanley had evacuated his office when the plane struck the North Tower, but when a security guard told him the South Tower was safe, he returned to his office on the eighty-first floor. A friend from Chicago, who was watching the unfolding events on television, called Stanley, begging him to leave. While he was on the phone, Stanley looked out his office window and saw United 175 coming directly at him. Realizing that the plane was going to hit the building, Stanley said a quick prayer and dove under his desk just seconds before the plane struck. The left wing sliced through his office and became lodged in a doorway twenty feet from his desk. The eighty-second floor collapsed, but Stanley's desk miraculously held up, and he was able to dig out from under it. However, he couldn't find a way to escape the floor. So he prayed, "Lord, send somebody, anybody to help me!" And then he began calling for help.

That's when Brian heard Stanley's plea: "I'm buried! I can't breathe. Is anyone there?"

Brian left his group and followed the sound of Stanley's voice, but a wall separated the two men. Brian yelled for Stanley to bang on the wall, so he could locate Stanley's exact whereabouts. Once he figured out where Stanley was, Brian noticed a gap at the top of the wall. If Stanley could climb it, Brian could pull him over. After a few unsuccessful attempts—and after injuring his hand on a nail—Stanley made it to the gap. Brian reached up and pulled Stanley over the wall. Falling backward into Brian's lap, Stanley said, "Hallelujah! I've been saved!"[2]

When Brian got back to the stairwell, his group was gone. He would later learn that they had climbed to the roof. Brian and Stanley, however, decided to climb down. Though they had to scramble over debris until they passed the seventy-seventh floor, they never encountered the fire the woman told Brian about.

Once on the ground, they ran from the building. When they reached Trinity Church, Stanley and Brian stopped and looked back toward the South Tower. Stanley said, "I think that building's gonna come down."

"I don't think so," Brian said. "That's a steel structure—" Before he could complete his thought, they heard the *boom, boom, boom* of the upper floors beginning to pancake down. Brian and Stanley ran into an office on Broadway just as the dust cloud enveloped the building. They exchanged business cards and talked about their families. Eventually, Brian found his way back home to New Jersey, and Stanley went to a hospital for his injured hand. Later that evening, Stanley called Brian to make sure he had made it home safely.

Two strangers thrown together by the events of that terrible day became lifelong friends—or "blood brothers," as they call themselves.[3]

Help Others

Brian and Stanley saved each other that day. Brian obviously saved Stanley by pulling him over the wall. But Stanley also saved Brian by his calls for help. If Brian hadn't heard Stanley's pleas, he might have gone to the roof with his coworkers and perished with them there. Each man, like Oskar Schindler, saved "the world entire" for the other.

When I read this story, I was inspired by Brian Clark because he exhibited a selflessness that is rarely seen these days. There are many stories of heroism from September 11, most of them about first responders who are trained to rush into crumbling buildings to save lives. But average citizens—bank executives like Brian Clark, for example—don't choose inherently dangerous professions, so their heroics are even more memorable.

When thrown into life-threatening situations, most of us tend to focus on self-preservation. Images from that day, of men and women running for their lives, prove the point. Dangerous circumstances tend to trigger a survival-of-the-fittest mentality. Most people focus on saving their own lives and let their companions fend for themselves. But that was not true of Brian Clark.

Those who help others during difficult times are able to shift their perspective from victim to rescuer. By doing so, they ensure better outcomes not only for others but often for themselves as well.

As followers of Jesus, you and I are called on to reject the attitude of selfishness. Even when we go through challenging times, we are not to turn our backs on others. Rather, God has given us the responsibility to help people wherever and whenever we can.

Jesus's Example of Helping Others

When Jesus had the opportunity to summarize His ministry on earth, He said, "The Son of Man did not come to be served, but to serve, and to give His life a ransom for many" (Matt. 20:28). Jesus was saying that His purpose was to help others by dying on the cross for our sins.

If Jesus had the same life purpose that most of us have—securing our own peace, prosperity, and pleasure—then He would have never given up the perks of heaven to come to earth. Think about this: before Jesus was born in Bethlehem, He existed in eternity past. Colossians 1 tells us that Jesus created the entire universe. And one day, when we are in heaven, we will bow down and worship Christ, singing, "Worthy is the Lamb" (Rev. 5:12). But right now, Jesus says the thing that He wants to be remembered for is not His majesty or His glory. He wants to be remembered as the One who came to serve others.

Just consider a few things that Jesus said about helping others. In Matthew 5:42, He said, "Give to the one who asks you, and do not turn away from the one who wants to borrow from you" (NIV). And in Matthew 23:11–12, Jesus said,

"The greatest among you will be your servant. For those who exalt themselves will be humbled, and those who humble themselves will be exalted" (NIV).

Perhaps nowhere else in Scripture is Jesus's attitude about helping others expressed more clearly than in Luke 10, which records the parable of the good Samaritan. You are probably familiar with the story. A man was traveling from Jerusalem to Jericho when he was ambushed by robbers and left for dead. A priest passed by and refused to render aid. Then a Levite walked by and offered no help. But a Samaritan took care of his need and made sure he was provided for. "Which of these three do you think proved to be a neighbor to the man who fell into the robbers' hands?" Jesus asked His listeners. "The one who showed mercy toward him," someone responded. Then Jesus said, "Go and do the same" (Luke 10:36–37).

In this parable, Jesus taught that our neighbor is anyone who is in need. For us to walk by somebody who is in need and neglect them is to sin against them.

If you and I want to know how to help others, we can imitate Jesus's example and actions. We are never more like Jesus than when we look for opportunities to help others.

What Does It Mean to Help Others?

Every day, we encounter people who have needs we are capable of meeting. And if you truly want to help others, then you are going to put the needs of others above your own needs.

Let's get specific. Husbands, for us to help others means to put our wife's need for conversation in the evening above our own need to unwind after a hard day. Wives, for you to help others means to put your husband's need for respect above your need to correct him. Parents, to help others means to put your children's need for a quality education above what you think is your need for early retirement. That's what serving others is. It is putting the needs of others above our own.

Let's be honest: helping others neither comes naturally nor does it come easily. From the time we draw our first breath, we are programmed to think, *Me, my, and mine.* It is part of the DNA we inherited from Adam to be selfish. You don't have to teach a child to be selfish, do you? And it doesn't get better the older we get. Since getting older is no guarantee that we will learn to place the needs of others above our own, then how can we learn to become better helpers?

A Plan to Help Others

In his letter to the Philippians, Paul used Jesus as the ultimate example of selflessness. Let's take a closer look at the three-step plan outlined in Philippians 2, modeled on the life of Jesus Christ, that teaches us how to develop the essential survival skill of helping others.

Remove Selfishness and Conceit from Your Life

First, Paul wrote, "Do nothing from selfishness or empty conceit" (Phil. 2:3). Obviously, this is easier said than done. As we have seen, our sinful human nature leans toward selfishness. Yet selfishness leads to a small life. Billy Graham once said, "The smallest package I ever saw was a man wrapped up wholly in himself."[4] Whenever we are more interested in meeting our own than meeting the needs of others, we are going to have trouble in our relationships.

For example, a husband comes home from work, and he is exhausted. He sits in his favorite chair, scrolls through his phone, and watches television while he is waiting for supper. His wife is busy fixing supper, and she says, "Honey, we're out of milk. Could you please run to the store and get a gallon?" He responds, "I'm too tired. I've been working all day." Now, he didn't mean to set off a nuclear explosion. It may have seemed like an innocent enough statement, but the husband was really saying, "My needs are more important than yours."

But when we come to faith in Christ, we become a "new creation" (2 Cor. 5:17 NIV). Scripture says that followers of Jesus "no longer live for [ourselves]," but we are able to live for others (v. 15). Jesus said that anybody who wants to be like Him "must deny [themselves], and take up [their] cross daily and follow [Him]" (Luke 9:23). In other words, if we are going to live out our Christian faith and survive the challenges of this world, you and I must daily put to death our selfish desires and ambitions and begin to focus on helping others.

I was recently talking to my friend Governor Mike Huckabee before we taped an interview for his popular talk show. He was telling me about the wonderful church he attends. "What do you do in the church?" I asked. He laughed and said, "I drive the golf cart around the parking lot, picking up people who need help getting to the church." Wow! Here's a popular television host, former governor, and a past contender for president of the United States who doesn't think it is beneath him to perform what many would consider a menial task. But it isn't menial because it is a necessary task—and it serves others. Governor Huckabee doesn't allow conceit or self-importance to prevent him from meeting the genuine needs of other people.

Regard Others as More Important Than Yourself

Second, Paul said, "With humility of mind regard one another as more important than yourselves" (Phil. 2:3). Now, you may be wondering, "Pastor, are you saying that we should *never* think of ourselves? Doesn't God want us to take care of ourselves?" Of course God wants us to take care of our basic needs and the needs of our families. In 1 Timothy 5:8, Paul said, "If anyone does not provide for his own, and especially for those of his household, he has denied the faith and is worse than an unbeliever." The Bible is clear that we are responsible to care for ourselves and our family members.

So Paul was not saying that we should have no regard for our own lives. Instead, we are to view others with greater consideration than we view ourselves. As Paul said in Romans 12:10, "Be devoted to one another in love. Honor one another above yourselves" (NIV). The key to helping others, especially during difficult times, is to regard others as more important than yourself.

Giving preference to one another doesn't always require extraordinary acts of heroism like Brian Clark's. It can be as simple as noticing someone and doing something kind for that person. Perhaps you could write a note expressing your appreciation or treat them to lunch at a restaurant of their choice.

Not long ago, I came across the story of a memorable demonstration of honor that took place on an American Airlines flight from Atlanta to Chicago. Among the passengers lining up to board the plane were nine US soldiers on leave from active duty overseas. A passenger approached one of the soldiers and offered to exchange his first-class ticket for the soldier's coach ticket. Inspired by the man's selfless act, other passengers traded their first-class seats for the coach seats occupied by the eight remaining soldiers. A flight attendant later expressed her gratitude for "two groups of unselfish people: those who would put their lives on the line to protect their fellow citizens' freedom, and those who were not ashamed to say thank you."[5] One man's small action spread to others and had lasting positive results.

What small action can you take to honor somebody in your life today? When you and I stop focusing exclusively on our needs and look around us, we can find many ways to regard others as more important than ourselves.

Relate to Others by Looking Out for Their Interests

Finally, Paul said, "Do not merely look out for your own personal interests, but also for the interests of others" (Phil. 2:4). Helping others simply means meeting the needs of other people. If we truly love other people, then we will put their interests above our own interests.

Think about it for a moment. Every day, we encounter people who have needs that we are capable of meeting. And if we have the attitude of Christ, then we are going to put the needs of these people above our own needs.

For example, for you to put the interests of others above your own, you might have to swallow your pride and admit to somebody that you were wrong. Or you might have to give up the money you set aside for some special purpose to meet the need of an aging parent, a child, or someone in the body of Christ. Possibly, you might have to give up your to-do list to be interrupted and meet the very real need of somebody God brings into your life. That's what it means to look out for the interests of others.

Barnabas: A Helper for the Early Church

Somebody who clearly understood the value of helping others was an unknown man from a faraway place who became a leader of the early church. Although his parents named him Joseph, history remembers him by the nickname given to him by the apostles: Barnabas, meaning "Son of Encouragement" (Acts 4:36). Because he continually encouraged the apostles by his positive words and helpful actions, every time the disciples saw Joseph coming, they said, "Here comes that Son of Encouragement!" (Those of us who are pastors sometimes have a different nickname for more bothersome church members!)

The Greek root of "encouragement" means "one who comes alongside," or, more simply, a "helper." Jesus used the same word to describe the Holy Spirit when He said to His disciples, "I will ask the Father, and He will give you another *Helper*, that He may be with you forever" (John 14:16). And in verse 26, He said, "But the *Helper*, the Holy Spirit, whom the Father will send in My name, He will teach you all things, and bring to your remembrance all that I said to you."

That's who Barnabas was—a helper. When we trace his life through the book of Acts, we discover at least three areas where Barnabas specifically helped others: with his money, as a mentor, and in his ministry.

Barnabas the Philanthropist

Luke said in Acts 4:36–37 that Barnabas sold a tract of land and gave the proceeds to the church at Jerusalem. The early church had a collective mindset when it came to their possessions. "Not one" member of the congregation, Luke wrote, "claimed that anything belonging to him was his own, but all things were common property to them" (v. 32). As a result, "There was not a needy person among them, for all who were owners of land or houses would sell them and bring the proceeds of the sales and lay them at the apostles' feet, and they would be distributed to each as any had need" (vv. 34–35).

If we are not careful, we might think the early church practiced a form of economic socialism, something Winston Churchill famously called "the equal sharing of miseries."[6] But we would be wrong in that conclusion. These early Christians did not liquidate everything they had and put it into a common fund. After all, you can only sell everything you own once! Instead, these Christians understood that the property belonging to them was really owned by God Himself. They were only caretakers, or stewards, of what belonged to God. God could ask them to surrender those possessions anytime there was a need in the church—which is why they held their possessions loosely.

If we look closely at Acts 4:32, the central idea is this: "The congregation of those who believed were of *one heart and soul*." Oneness of purpose is what motivated these believers to such generosity. If they had pooled their resources out of obligation, it's doubtful Luke would have described them as being of "one heart and soul." Besides, there would be no reason to point out Barnabas's generosity if he was merely doing his required duty.

The apostles taught that personal property was just that—personal. In the story of Ananias and Sapphira, Peter said, "Ananias, why has Satan filled your heart to lie to the Holy Spirit and to keep back some of the price of the land? While it remained unsold, did it not *remain your own*? And after it was sold, was it not *under your control*?" (5:3–4). Ananias and Sapphira were severely disciplined not because they failed to give all the proceeds to the church but because they lied to the Holy Spirit.

But Barnabas gave generously to help meet the needs of those in the congregation. He lived out "the words of the Lord Jesus, [who] said, 'It is more blessed to give than to receive'" (20:35). In many ways, generosity is its own reward.

Another generous helper, a seventy-four-year-old New Jersey man named Joseph Badame, would agree. Badame and his wife, Phyliss, spent decades stockpiling supplies in their doomsday bunker, including coal furnaces, survivalist books, and several three-hundred-pound barrels—each filled with enough dry food to sustain eighty-four people for four months. After his wife passed away, Badame was heartbroken. He described himself as "a spirit in search of a purpose." Then he met a Puerto Rican couple—and he had an idea for his stockpile. He donated almost all of the food to assist with Puerto Rico disaster relief. "Phyliss and I prepared all this for one group of people," he said. "And it turns out it's going to help another group of people. That's wonderful." His act of generosity not only helped families affected by Hurricane Maria in Puerto Rico but also gave Badame a new purpose in life—one that embraces the survival strategy of helping others.[7]

Barnabas the Mentor

In the first century, Christianity was a dangerous belief—especially in Jerusalem, the capital of Judaism. The church was just days or weeks old when persecution began. First came the imprisonment of Peter and John, followed by the stoning of Stephen, followed by widespread and organized oppression under Saul. While he was on one such persecution mission to Damascus, Saul was miraculously converted after seeing and speaking with the risen Jesus.

Having lost his sight after his encounter with the Lord, Saul fasted and prayed for three days. On the third day, the Lord commanded a believer named Ananias to go to Saul, touch his eyes, and heal him. Considering the fact that Saul had a reputation for killing Christians, Ananias was understandably afraid to go! But in obedience to the Lord, Ananias courageously went to help Saul.

Saul then retreated to the desert of Arabia for three years before returning to Damascus, where he began "to proclaim Jesus in the synagogues" and "confounding the Jews . . . by proving that this Jesus is the Christ" (Acts 9:20, 22). When the Jews in Damascus tried to kill Saul, he escaped to Jerusalem, where he tried to connect with the disciples. Like

Ananias, the disciples were understandably afraid of Saul. They had heard about his preaching, but what if it was a trick to spy on Christians to gain information to persecute them?

"But Barnabas . . ." (v. 27). What an encouragement for Saul! Barnabas wasn't afraid. He bravely took Saul to the apostles and became his advocate. Barnabas assured the apostles that Saul had seen the Lord, spoken with Him, and proclaimed the gospel. Based on this recommendation, Saul was accepted into the Jerusalem church, where he ministered freely, "speaking out boldly in the name of the Lord" (v. 28). And when the Jews in Jerusalem tried to kill him, Saul's new friends paid for his passage to his hometown of Tarsus.

It seems that every time Barnabas showed up in the New Testament, he was helping and encouraging someone. And perhaps nowhere was his commitment to help others on display more than in the lives of Saul (Paul) and John Mark.

Most of us know John Mark as the author of the Gospel that bears his name, Mark. But Colossians 4:10 tells us he was also Barnabas's cousin. Barnabas and Paul invited John Mark along on their missionary journey, but after weeks of walking, sleeping in all sorts of weather, and fighting off fatigue and bugs and pagans, John Mark had had enough. He "left them and returned to Jerusalem" (Acts 13:13).

Fast-forward a couple of chapters. Paul and Barnabas had returned from their missionary journey and were back in Antioch ministering together. After they traveled to Jerusalem to help settle a theological controversy, Acts 15:36 tells us that Paul proposed a return trip to the Gentile churches to see how things were faring. Barnabas thought that was a wonderful idea. He suggested they take John Mark along with them.

I imagine the following conversation went something like this: "No way am I going to take that snot-nosed deserter with me," Paul said.

"Yes, he's young and inexperienced. And no one is denying that he failed when the going got tough," Barnabas responded. "But John Mark deserves a second chance, just as you did—in case you've forgotten! How do you expect him to learn and grow if you aren't willing to mentor him, encourage him, and help him?"

The two men were at an impasse, so they separated. Paul took Silas north, and Barnabas took John Mark south.

Both men were right about John Mark—he *had* deserted them, and he *did* deserve a second chance. Fortunately, the separation of ministry didn't mean a separation of relationship. Mark flourished under Barnabas's help, becoming a valuable servant of Christ. In fact, years later, while Paul was awaiting execution in Rome, he wrote Timothy, "Pick up Mark and bring him with you, for he is useful to me for service" (2 Tim. 4:11). Mark evidently grew and became valuable to the early church because of Barnabas's help and encouragement.

What do you see in the people around you? Do you tend to define others by their failures, or do you see the potential for their future? Is there somebody in your community or church who could benefit from a second chance? If so, take the risk to be the kind of mentor who invests in those people and helps them. You never know who the next John Mark will be!

Barnabas the Minister

When word traveled to Jerusalem that Gentiles in Antioch had come to faith in Jesus, the church leaders sent Barnabas to Antioch to investigate. Why did they send Barnabas, instead of one of the apostles? Barnabas was from Cyprus and had spent a significant part of his life dealing with Greek-speaking Gentiles, so he was best suited to the language and the culture.

What Barnabas found in Antioch was amazing. "The hand of the Lord was with them," and he "witnessed the grace of God" upon them (Acts 11:21, 23). Barnabas encouraged the believers there, urging them "to remain true to the Lord" (v. 23).

Through the ministry of Barnabas, "considerable numbers were brought to the Lord" (v. 24). Because of the explosive growth of the church in that city, Barnabas knew he needed a partner in ministry. So he went to Tarsus and found Saul (later known as Paul) and "brought him to Antioch" (vv. 25–26). They ministered together in that city until they were commissioned as missionaries to the Gentiles.

Early in their travels, Luke recorded their activities as "Barnabas and Saul." But in time, it became apparent that Paul was the leader of the group, so Luke changed the order to "Paul and Barnabas." I think it's interesting that nowhere do we read that Barnabas was jealous of Paul's increasing leadership and ministry. In fact, this was why Barnabas took the risk in mentoring Paul. Barnabas saw something unique in the man, something necessary for the spread of the gospel.

When Ronald Reagan was president, he had a sign on his desk meant to keep egos in check. In fact, when I visited the

ᵣrary a few years ago, I purchased a replica of this
ı now sits on my desk as well. It says, "There is no
ᵢat a man can do or where he can go if he doesn't
ᵐⁱⁿᵈ ....ᵢ gets the credit." Barnabas lived and ministered
by this motto.

Practical Tips for Helping Others

None of us can survive an increasingly hostile culture or the
difficulties of everyday life without a Barnabas. Somewhere
along the way, God has placed a Barnabas in your path—
perhaps a parent or relative, a friend, a teacher, a coworker,
or a boss. We ought to be grateful for every person who has
encouraged and mentored us.

What about you? Are you somebody's Barnabas? Chances
are, there is a person in your life whom you can encourage
and help. As you pray for God to show you somebody to
whom you can be a Barnabas, let's look at three practical
tips for helping others.

Value Other People

Pastors sometimes joke, "Ministry would be great if it
wasn't for the people." Of course, that is what ministry is all
about—sharing the good news of Jesus Christ with others.
But let's face it: some people can be annoying, stubborn,
and downright nasty. But they are also made in the image of
God. Our job is to see them as God sees them—as so valuable that Christ died for them. As C. S. Lewis pointed out,
"There are no *ordinary* people. You have never talked to a

mere mortal. Nations, cultures, arts, civilisations—these are mortal, and their life is to ours as the life of a gnat. But it is immortals whom we joke with, work with, marry, snub, and exploit—immortal horrors or everlasting splendours."[8] Everybody we encounter is an eternal soul.

We value others by seeking opportunities to serve them by placing their needs and interests ahead of our own. It doesn't have to be big and complicated. Open a door for someone. Cook dinner—and then wash the dishes afterward. Take a lonely friend out for a cup of coffee, or offer to mow the lawn of an elderly neighbor. You get the idea. When you see others as valuable, you will treat them as valuable.

Champion the Underdog

Most of us can remember the kid on the playground who always got picked last for red rover or kickball. You might have even been that kid. If so, you know the pain of rejection, the loneliness of being the outsider, and the anger that arises from being made fun of or bullied.

Underdogs have a tough time thriving because they are focused on simply surviving. Few people need a helping hand from a Barnabas more than those who are being perpetually kicked and knocked down.

Again and again in the Bible, we see God championing the underdog. God repeatedly chose younger sons such as Abel, Joseph, and David instead of the oldest son. God chose the fledgling nation of Israel instead of a powerful nation like Babylon, Assyria, or Egypt. Even God's own Son, Jesus, came to earth not as a mighty king in a palace but as a helpless baby in a barn. I agree with author Philip Yancey, who

221

observed, "As I read the birth stories about Jesus I cannot help but conclude that though the world may be tilted toward the rich and powerful, God is tilted toward the underdog."[9]

If you have experience being the underdog, then showing compassion and helping others probably comes more easily for you. Your heart already has a soft spot for those who are overlooked or outcast. But if you have always been popular, championing underdogs may be more difficult. Part of the reason is that when you were younger (and maybe even now), you were the one pushing underdogs around. But since Christ has gotten hold of your life, you realize that your former perspective was wrong. Nevertheless, you may still be struggling with those old feelings and thoughts. What can you do to make a permanent change?

Carefully consider Paul's admonishment in Philippians 2:5–8:

Have this attitude in yourselves which was also in Christ Jesus, who, although He existed in the form of God, did not regard equality with God a thing to be grasped, but emptied Himself, taking the form of a bond-servant, and being made in the likeness of men. Being found in appearance as a man, He humbled Himself by becoming obedient to the point of death, even death on a cross.

Ask God to change your heart and mind into these Christ-like attitudes. A word of warning, though: if you get serious about this, be prepared for the Lord to answer your prayer. He might have you track down those you have hurt in the past and ask for forgiveness. But He will also give you a new capacity for compassion that will cause you to want to help others.

Offer Second Chances

If you are going to love people, you are going to be disappointed. It comes with the territory. People can never be completely trustworthy. They will fail you, abandon you, and sin against you. But that's no reason to retreat into a hermitlike existence. That's not our calling. God expects us to "go into all the world" and engage with others (Mark 16:15). Yet it is discouraging when others disappoint us. So how do we overcome our disappointments and give others a second chance?

Let's be realistic. When it came to John Mark, for example, Barnabas was concerned about the man; Paul was concerned about the mission. Both were important. It would be foolish to loan money to a friend who is already in your debt. It's equally foolish to buy your son a new car after he carelessly wrecked his last car. On the other hand, we should not refuse to help people when they are in real need. Remember, God is the God of second chances. He's the God of grace and justice, holding us accountable and offering help when we are in need.

The trick is finding the right balance between grace and justice. This was where Paul and Barnabas got it wrong. John Mark didn't have to go on their second trip, but he didn't have to be left behind either. He could have been assigned a role in the church at Antioch or been taken part of the way on the journey and then reevaluated. People who fail need to be given second chances. Let's not forget: we have all been given a second chance. But more than that, we have been given "the ministry of reconciliation" with others (2 Cor. 5:18).

Let me wrap up this chapter with an observation from psychiatrist Carl Menninger. When Dr. Menninger was asked what he would do if he knew he was on the verge of a nervous breakdown, he said, "I'd go out, find somebody in need, and help him."[10] That's good advice. Whenever we are going through difficult times in this hostile world, let's look around us and have the courage to help somebody, just like Barnabas . . . and just like Jesus.

Do the Next Right Thing

Vice Admiral James Stockdale had a brush with fame as Texas billionaire H. Ross Perot's running mate on the independent Reform Party ticket. On October 13, 1992, his first words during the nationally televised vice-presidential debate were "Who am I? What am I doing here?" The questions were meant to introduce himself, but instead made him a laughingstock in the media, who portrayed Stockdale as a weak, doddering old man—someone from a bygone era, out of step with the times, and fodder for jokes on late-night television.

Stockdale may have been from a bygone era, but he was far from doddering. A graduate of the US Naval Academy, Stockdale was an accomplished fighter pilot. In 1965, the forty-one-year-old father of four was shot down over Vietnam. As he ejected from his A-4 Skyhawk and floated to the ground, he said to himself, "Five years." That's how long he thought he would be in captivity. As it turned out, he spent almost eight years in Hoa Lo Prison—the infamous "Hanoi Hilton." For four of those years, he was in solitary confinement. For two years, he was forced to wear leg irons. He was tortured at least fifteen times.

Stockdale was the highest-ranking officer among the hundreds of US prisoners of war in the prison camp. Despite his solitary confinement, Stockdale organized a system of wall taps, hand signals, and hidden notes for the prisoners to communicate with one another. He also developed a set of rules governing prisoner behavior. These rules gave his fellow American prisoners a sense of purpose and hope. "When a person is alone in a cell and sees the door open only once or twice a day for a bowl of soup," Stockdale recalled years later, "he has to build some sort of ritual into his life if he wants to avoid becoming an animal."

Stockdale led the prisoners' resistance against Vietnamese attempts to use them as propaganda or informants on fellow Americans. To Stockdale, integrity was the most important thing to maintain for a prisoner of war—more important than food, avoiding torture, or life itself. He wrote, "I came to realize . . . that if you don't lose integrity you can't be had and you can't be hurt."[1]

To live as "honorable prisoners," Stockdale instructed the American soldiers that it was okay to divulge useless information along with their name, rank, serial number, and birth date. One pilot, under torture, gave his captors the names of comic book heroes when they asked for the names of top flyers. In doing so, he bolstered the men's spirits, protected vital military secrets, and preserved his honor.

In 1969, Stockdale's Vietnamese captors decided to parade the prisoners through the streets of downtown Hanoi, to show foreign journalists how "humanely" the prisoners were being treated. Stockdale refused to take part in this propaganda charade. He slashed his scalp with a razor and beat his face with a wooden stool, because he knew his captors wouldn't want to show a prisoner with cuts and bruises on his face. When he learned that some prisoners had died during torture, Stockdale cut his wrists to let his captors know that he would rather die than betray his country, his countrymen, and his character.

These were radical steps to take to protect his integrity and the honor of his men. But they worked. When the Vietnamese saw how determined Stockdale was to resist, and how his resistance emboldened his fellow prisoners, they ceased torturing American POWs and improved conditions in the prison.

In 1973, during Operation Homecoming, Stockdale, along with the other prisoners in the Hanoi Hilton, was finally released. His courage and heroism became widely known, and in 1976, President Gerald Ford awarded Stockdale the Congressional Medal of Honor.

Do the Next Right Thing

James Stockdale embodied the final survival strategy we will look at in this book: do the next right thing. When his plane was hit by antiaircraft fire, Stockdale didn't waste time thinking about all the things he could have done differently to avoid the situation he was in. He didn't blame others—after all, the North Vietnamese soldiers were doing their jobs. And he didn't wallow in self-pity.

Instead, he simply focused on doing the next right thing. Every day in prison, Stockdale made choices that maintained his integrity and enabled him to resist collaborating with the enemy. And he looked for ways to help and encourage the other prisoners. In this way, he was able to survive what ended up being one of the longest imprisonments in one of the most horrific prison camps in history.

Years later, business expert Jim Collins interviewed Stockdale for his book *Good to Great*. When asked to describe his strategy for surviving the Hanoi Hilton, Stockdale responded, "I never lost faith in the end of the story. I never doubted not only that I would get out, but also that I would prevail in the end and turn the experience into the defining event of my life, which, in retrospect, I would not trade."[2]

Stockdale went on to explain that the prisoners who didn't make it out of Vietnam were those who kept looking for an upcoming rescue instead of doing what was necessary in the present. As a result, they were continually disappointed when anticipated rescue dates didn't come, and they eventually died of a broken heart. "This is a very important lesson," Stockdale concluded. "You must never confuse faith that you will prevail in the end—which you can never afford to lose—with the discipline to confront the most brutal facts of your current reality, whatever they might be."[3]

A student of philosophy, Stockdale understood that life isn't always fair. He also realized that he couldn't control everything, so he chose to focus on only the things he could control. He liked to quote the ancient philosopher Epictetus: "Some things are under our control, while others are not under our control."[4]

During his time as a prisoner of war, Stockdale didn't get overwhelmed or lose sight of what was important. Rather, he broke events into simple, manageable tasks so he could

take organized, decisive action, which cleared]
confidence, and cut through the chaos. This i‚
to do the next right thing.

We don't have to experience what James ‚..
lose sight of what is most important in life. Whenever we face
difficult circumstances, we can become overwhelmed and feel
as if we are stuck in a helpless situation from which we cannot escape. You may not be in a literal prison, as Stockdale
was, but perhaps you feel stuck in a prison of depression,
resentment, anxiety, or fear. Or maybe you feel trapped in
a dead-end job, a difficult marriage, singleness, aging, or a
culture that is increasingly hostile to your Christian beliefs
and values. The good news is that no matter how difficult or
hopeless your circumstances may seem right now, you can
take the necessary steps to make a better life for yourself and
for those around you.

In other words: do all the good you can, where you can,
while you can.

What Does It Mean to "Do Good"?

In Galatians 6:9–10, the apostle Paul said, "Let us not lose
heart in doing good, for in due time we will reap if we do
not grow weary. So then, while we have opportunity, let us
do good to all people, and especially to those who are of
the household of the faith." How does doing the next right
thing—or, as Paul put it, "doing good"—enable us to avoid
becoming weary?

In Greek, the phrase "growing weary" refers to more than
just physical fatigue; it carries the idea of becoming exhausted

to the point of giving up. It was used to describe a bowstring that had become unstrung; it was limp and useless. As any violinist knows, bowstrings must be taut to function properly. In a similar way, you and I can become virtually useless in the ministry God has called us to when our shoulders sag in despair and we are too weary to go on.

To survive in this challenging world, we must have the courage to take the next step, whatever it may be, to get up and get going to fulfill our God-given calling. As Paul put it in 1 Corinthians 15:58, we are to be "steadfast, immovable, always abounding in the work of the Lord, knowing that [our] toil is not in vain in the Lord."

Why Should We "Do Good"?

Now, as we talk in this chapter about the importance of doing good, I want to make sure this biblical truth is crystal clear: we are not saved *by* good works, but we are saved *for* good works.

In Ephesians 2:8–9, Paul explained that our salvation is a gift received by grace through faith in Jesus Christ: "By grace you have been saved through faith; and that not of yourselves, it is a gift of God; not as a result of works, so that no one may boast." Then in verse 10, Paul went on to say, "We are His workmanship, *created in Christ Jesus for good works*, which God prepared beforehand so that we would walk in them." While "doing good" doesn't save us, God saved us so that we could spend the rest of our lives doing good.

You see, the reason Jesus Christ died on the cross for you and me was not just to give us a free pass to heaven. He came to give us a whole new way of living that would result in producing good works. As we keep doing the next right thing, Jesus rewards us with a life that is rich, satisfying, and fulfilling. As He said in John 10:10, "I came that they may have life, and have it abundantly."

There are many ways that you and I can "do good" to serve God, help others, and expand God's kingdom. Perhaps you could volunteer in the church nursery (a service that some might even say is worthy of a medal!). Maybe for you, "doing good" would involve caring for an ailing or elderly parent. Or perhaps you could take a meal to your new neighbors as a way of doing the next right thing. Mowing the lawn of the widow down the street, visiting a friend in the hospital, offering encouragement to a coworker, washing the dishes for your family, taking your kids on vacation—all of these acts, and a thousand more, fulfill the biblical command to do good.

When Should We "Do Good"?

Paul said that God gives us the opportunity to do good, but the time to do good is limited. He told the Galatians, "So then, while we have opportunity, let us do good" (6:10). And in Ephesians 5:16, Paul wrote, "[Make] the most of every opportunity" (NIV). This phrase literally means "buy back the time." We are to invest our days, weeks, and years in the things that matter for eternity.

Paul could have used the phrase made popular by Robin Williams's character in the movie *Dead Poets Society*: "*Carpe diem*—seize the day." Don't put off opportunities to do good

231

for another time. Have the courage to act now! Grab the moment and make the most of it! Why? Because those opportunities to do good will not always be available.

I once read that when Walt Disney was making plans to build Disneyland, he offered a friend the opportunity to buy the surrounding land, since he knew it would greatly increase in value. But the friend hesitated to take the offer, saying he needed to think about it. Unfortunately, he waited too long. Because Disney needed an answer quickly, his friend lost the opportunity, along with vast wealth.[5]

It is important for us to take advantage of the opportunities God gives us. For one reason, the return of Christ is closer than ever before. People all around us are hurting and in need of the gospel, and our opportunity has never been greater to reach them for Christ. As Billy Graham observed, "Today's world is said to be multiplying crises all around us. But we must never forget that, for the gospel, each crisis is an opportunity."[6]

But there's another reason you and I need to seize opportunities to do good. Regardless of when Christ returns, our time on earth is limited; therefore, our opportunity to do good is limited. In my desk drawer at home, I have an envelope filled with gift cards to various restaurants and stores that people have given me for special occasions. Recently, I retrieved one of those cards to take my family out to eat. When the waiter presented me with the check, I gave him the gift card. A few moments later, he returned and discreetly whispered, "I'm sorry, but your gift card has expired." I wished I had used that card before its value disappeared!

Before your time or your opportunities to "do good" vanish like a vapor, what opportunities would you like to seize?

How to Make the Most of Our Opportunities

There are three ways we can make the most of our opportunities to do good. First, *look beyond yourself.* We looked at this in depth in chapter 9, so we don't need to go into too much detail here, but the Bible commands us to consider the needs of others (Phil. 2:3–4). I love this quote I heard from my friend Bobb Biehl: "Every life exists for one of two purposes: to fill a greed or to meet a need." If you are serious about being others-focused instead of self-focused, then you don't have to look far or hard to see genuine needs. Everywhere you look, there are people in need. See what must be done, and then do it.

How about the kids in your neighborhood—do they need tutoring or school supplies or a coach for their baseball team? Does a single mom or widow in your church need home repair, or does your local library need someone to read to children? Could your community food pantry use some help sorting donated items, or would a nearby crisis pregnancy center appreciate someone to organize a baby shower for teenage mothers? Do you have the means and time to meet one or more of those needs? Consider if there is something you could do to help others with your unique talent or spiritual gift. (If you need help thinking of ideas, call your church and ask about ministry opportunities.) Then do the next right thing, and meet that need if you have the ability to do so. As you look for opportunities God may be giving you, be sure to keep this in mind: many people don't recognize opportunity because it often comes disguised as hard work.

Second, *ask the Lord to create opportunities*. Maybe you live in an affluent neighborhood where you don't see many needs. When is the last time you asked God to create opportunities for you to do the next right thing? Paul did. He asked the Colossian Christians to pray "that God will open up to us a door for the word, so that we may speak forth the mystery of Christ" (Col. 4:3). If it was good enough for the apostle Paul to ask the Lord to create opportunities for doing good, then it's good enough for you and me. But be warned: this is a prayer the Lord *loves* to answer!

One more note: opportunities often come in the form of interruptions. You may be motivated, energized, and ready to tackle your to-do list for the day when a phone call, a drop-in visit, or some other unanticipated event sabotages your schedule.

I am reminded of Jesus's parable of the good Samaritan in Luke 10:30–37. The Samaritan traveler refused to allow personal inconvenience to limit his sacrifice. This Samaritan was on a journey. He was not just riding around on his donkey looking for something to do! He was a wealthy man, so he was probably conducting important business. But he was willing to sacrifice his schedule to meet someone's real need. What do you and I have on our calendars that is so important we can't stop and help someone in need?

As we read the New Testament, we discover that many of Jesus's miracles were interruptions in His schedule. Jesus was on His way someplace else when He stopped and healed the man who had been blind since birth. Jesus was on His way to do something important when He stopped and healed the woman with the issue of blood. Jesus was in the middle of a sermon when a paralytic was lowered down from the ceiling. Jesus stopped, healed the man, and gave one of His greatest messages on forgiveness. We should never allow personal inconvenience to limit our sacrifice.

Although I have experienced many divine interruptions during the years I have been in the ministry, one unexpected opportunity in particular stands out to me. Several years ago, on a Friday afternoon, I mapped out what I was going to do on Monday: finish writing a chapter for a book, research the material for Sunday's sermon, conduct our staff meeting, and visit two prospects for our church. However, a phone call on Sunday evening changed all that. A man from a previous church informed me that his wife had passed away and requested that I conduct her memorial service. For a microsecond, I was perturbed at the prospect of not accomplishing what I had planned in the coming week. But that slight aggravation quickly evaporated as I remembered everything that this man and his wife had done for me through the years, and so I quickly accepted his invitation.

Even though that funeral service was not on my calendar, it was on God's. He knew where I needed to be. Not only did I have a chance to minister to people who were in need but I was also ministered to through love and encouragement from the members of that former church who were cherished friends. I returned home refreshed by the experience and thankful that the Lord had given me this opportunity to help others.

Third, *seize the opportunities that come.* We need to be prepared to make the most of the opportunities that come our way. When the Lord gives you an opportunity, jump in with both feet and trust Him to take care of the resources. Sometimes we give to those who are in need, and it comes back to us. But many times it never comes back to us. Yet that doesn't mean we shouldn't give of our time, talents, and treasure. The Bible teaches us to seize opportunities to help those in need. As Paul said in 2 Corinthians 9:8, "God is able to make all grace abound to you, so that always having all sufficiency in everything, you may have an abundance for every good deed."

For most Christians, our problem is not that we have too few opportunities for good deeds but too many. To keep from spreading ourselves and our resources too thin, we should get involved in the ones we truly believe the Lord is placing on our hearts. Specifically, which needs do you see that you feel passionate about? Which needs do you see that you possess the ability or gifts to meet? Philippians 2:13 reminds us that "it is God who is at work within you, giving you the will and the power to achieve his purpose" (Phillips). If God is calling us to meet a specific need, then He will give us both the desire ("will") and the ability ("power") to do so.

We shouldn't feel guilty for letting some opportunities pass by; other members of the body of Christ can take care of them. We can't do it all. Neither could Paul. Acts 16:7 tells us that during his second missionary journey, Paul wanted to go to the region of Bithynia (present-day Turkey), but "the Spirit of Jesus did not permit" it. Instead, God gave Paul a vision of an opportunity to preach in Macedonia. Did the people in Bithynia need the gospel? Absolutely! So did the people in Macedonia. But Bithynia wasn't Paul's opportunity; Macedonia was.

I remember a time when God made it clear that I was not to seize a specific opportunity. Many years ago, I was a youth minister. One day, the pastor of a well-known church called and said, "Robert, I'd like you to be our executive pastor." I thought, *This is a way to get me closer to my goal of being a senior pastor!* So I flew to that city, met with the pastor, and he said, "We want you to come. I'll contact you after I work things out with the personnel committee."

I went home ready to start packing my bags. The pastor eventually did call back as he promised, but not with the results I expected. He said, "We are going through some turmoil in our church, and it wouldn't be fair to bring you into this situation." As it turned out, within a few months he was gone as pastor of that church. Talk about being disappointed! Not only because I was confined to my present situation, but I thought, *God, what kind of cruel trick are You playing on me?* As I look back on that situation many years later, I realize God closed that door of opportunity because He was preparing the way for another opportunity for me: serving as the pastor of a small church that would eventually lead me to be senior pastor of First Baptist Church of Dallas.

Think about this: when you stand before the judgment seat of Christ to give an account of your life, God is not going to ask you, "Why didn't you take advantage of the opportunities I gave to Billy Graham?" God hasn't given most of us the gifts or opportunities that Billy Graham had. Instead, God is going to judge you according to how you have been faithful in the opportunities and gifts that, in His sovereignty, He has bestowed upon *you*.

The Lord gave Bithynia to others. He gave Macedonia to Paul. He gave the pastorate of First Baptist Dallas to me. And He will give an opportunity to you, if you are willing to obey the command to "do good to all people, and especially to those who are of the household of the faith" (Gal. 6:10).

Esther: A Woman Who Did the Next Right Thing

Tucked within the pages of the Bible are wonderful stories of women, many of whom are extraordinary examples of doing the next right thing. One of the greatest biblical role models is Queen Esther, whom I want my daughters and granddaughter to emulate because she was a woman of great faith, perseverance, and courage.

Esther was an orphan who was adopted by her older cousin Mordecai. Because she was "beautiful of form and face" (Esther 2:7), she was taken to the palace when the king of Persia (present-day Iran), Xerxes, was looking for a new bride. Esther not only "found favor in the eyes of all who saw her" (v. 15), but more significantly, she found favor with the king. The Bible says, "The king loved Esther more than all the women, and she found favor and kindness with him more than all the virgins, so that he set the royal crown on her head and made her queen" (v. 17).

Overnight, young Esther became the queen of Persia. But Esther had a secret: she was a Jew—a crime that became punishable by death, thanks to one of King Xerxes's royal officials, Haman. One day, Mordecai had refused to bow and pay homage to Haman as he demanded. Outraged, Haman persuaded the king to pass a law ordering not just Mordecai but all the Jews in Persia to be killed on a certain day.

The "Next Right Thing" for Esther

People in the ancient world, and in some Middle Eastern cultures today, mourn both verbally and visually. They wail and fall on the ground to demonstrate their grief. That's what Mordecai did after learning about the king's edict. Esther 4:1 tells us that he tore his clothes and put on a garment of goat's hair called sackcloth, threw ashes on his head, and "wailed loudly and bitterly." This extreme mourning spread throughout the land: "In each and every province where the command and decree of the king came, there was great mourning among the Jews, with fasting, weeping and wailing; and many lay on sackcloth and ashes" (v. 3).

Esther, however, knew nothing of the king's decree to kill her people. With her servants and bodyguards, the young queen lived in a bubble of luxury, well protected from the concerns of common people. When her servants told her that Mordecai was in mourning, Esther "writhed in great anguish" (v. 4). She sent him clean clothes, so he might come to the palace and tell her what was wrong. But Mordecai refused. Instead, he told Esther's servant Hathach about the king's order to kill the Jews. Mordecai gave Hathach a copy of the edict and asked him to show it to the queen.

Mordecai then made a request that he knew would put Esther's life in danger, because it would reveal her secret identity—that she too was a Jew. Through Hathach, Mordecai ordered Esther to "go in to the king to implore his favor and to plead with him for her people" (v. 8).

Mordecai's request put Queen Esther in a difficult spot. If she didn't do anything, her people would face a holocaust. But if she appeared before the king uninvited, she could be killed. Persian law said that if a person appeared before the king without being summoned, the king could withhold his golden scepter, and the person would die. But if he held out his golden scepter, then his visitor would live.

In other words, if Esther agreed to Mordecai's request, she had a 50/50 chance of life or death. So she told Mordecai that the gamble was too great.

Mordecai, however, wouldn't take no for an answer. First, he appealed to her common sense. He sent back a message to Esther: "Do not imagine that you in the king's palace can escape any more than all the Jews" (v. 13). The king's order was that all Jews, including women and children, must be killed. Esther couldn't keep her Jewish identity a secret forever. It was bound to come out sometime; why not now?

Next, Mordecai appealed to her conscience. Mordecai continued, "If you remain silent at this time, relief and deliverance will arise for the Jews from another place" (v. 14). In effect, Mordecai was saying, "It is outrageous for you to live a life of luxury in the palace while your people are dying in the streets." Even if she chose to remain silent, Mordecai believed God would send a deliverer. However, he said to her, "you and your father's house" might not survive the coming slaughter (v. 14).

Finally, Mordecai appealed to her calling. He asked her, "Who knows whether you have not attained royalty for such a time as this?" (v. 14). Could it be that God had brought Esther to the palace for this very purpose—to be the heroine who saved all of Israel?

Esther: A Profile in Courage

Mordecai's plea persuaded his cousin. Esther courageously decided to go in to see the king unannounced. But before she did, she asked Mordecai to have the Jews living in the capital city fast for three days; she and her maidens would join them. Then she would walk into the king's chamber, having resolved in her heart, "If I perish, I perish" (v. 16).

Esther didn't die that day. Instead, King Xerxes was pleased to see her and told her she could have anything she asked for. Esther already had a plan: she invited the king and Haman to attend two banquets, one that day and one the following day.

I don't know why Esther didn't reveal her Jewish identity at the first banquet, but the hand of God was clearly guiding her. The next day, King Xerxes and Haman attended Esther's second banquet, where she revealed that she was a Jew and asked the king to preserve her people from the edict dictating their annihilation. When Xerxes asked who had plotted such evil, she said, "A foe and an enemy is this wicked Haman!" (7:6).

Enraged, the king had Haman hanged. Though Persian law prevented him from overturning the previous edict, King Xerxes issued a new decree allowing the Jews to defend themselves on the appointed day of the massacre. Mordecai was promoted to prime minister, and Esther continued to serve as queen of Persia—the heroine of her people, all because she had the courage to do the next right thing.

Four Steps to Doing the Next Right Thing

You may never be called upon to do something as heroic as surviving as a prisoner of war or saving an entire race of people. But none of us is exempt from doing the next right thing in life. Whether it is deciding to take a new job, move to a new city, marry the person you're dating, start a family, care for aging parents, place your kids into public school or pull them out from public school, find a new church, confront a sinning friend or your own sin, wait patiently for God to work in the life of your rebellious child, or a thousand other decisions large and small, each one requires right action.

Using Esther as our model, let's look at four biblical steps in the process of doing the next right thing.

Step 1: Determine to Take Action Despite Danger or Doubt

It has been said that the two most important days in your life are the day you were born and the day you discover *why* you were born. Esther discovered why she was born—why she was made queen—on the day Mordecai said to her, "Who knows whether you have not attained royalty for such a time as this?" (Esther 4:14). Her purpose was to save the lives of her people.

Like Esther, many of us know we need to take a stand, even if it means leaving our comfort zones to shine the light of Christ in a dark world. How will you respond when God calls you to do the next right thing to expand His kingdom? Will you have the courage to move forward in faith? Esther determined to take action despite the dangers. This is the first step in doing the next right thing.

We also must do the next right thing despite any doubt we have about the outcome. Some years ago, I received an invitation to appear on Bill Maher's show *Real Time* on HBO. Knowing Bill's reputation for devouring Christians, I hesitated about accepting the invitation. I didn't want to embarrass myself—and by extension, the body of Christ—by looking foolish before millions of people. But I sensed God telling me that I needed to take advantage of this opportunity to be a witness to millions of people who might never darken the door of a church. So I accepted the invitation—even if it meant "perishing" on national television!

Amazingly, the interview went far better than I could have dreamed. At first, the audience booed some of my answers to the host's questions. But then something changed. The audience started laughing at some of my jokes and even applauding my answers to questions about the essence of the Christian message. After the show, the producer told me he had never seen Bill treat a Christian with as much respect as he had treated me.

Today—almost ten years later—people still stop me on the street and tell me they saw that interview and remember some of the things that I said. In spite of the very real doubts I had, I seized a unique opportunity God gave me . . . and He protected me.

When we know what needs to be done, we can't let fear, doubt, or the opinions of others keep us from doing the next right thing.

Step 2: Enlist Others in Our Action Plan

Though Esther resolved to take action, she wasn't reckless or careless. She didn't barge into King Xerxes's throne room, throw caution to the wind, and demand he save her people. Instead, she asked Mordecai and her fellow Jews to fast and pray for three days. During those days, she developed her plan and found the courage to carry it out.

When I decided to appear on Maher's television show, I immediately enlisted the help of three hundred of my prayer partners to pray before and during the interview. I knew that beyond an entertaining battle between a liberal talk show host and a conservative pastor, there was going to be a spiritual battle between the kingdom of light and the kingdom of darkness. I didn't want to walk into that studio without plenty of prayer cover for that battle!

Proverbs 15:22 says, "Without consultation, plans are frustrated, but with many counselors they succeed." That's worth remembering when we are considering whether to move forward with an opportunity to do good. We don't have to face decisions alone.

Some decisions we must make are easy, such as what to eat for lunch. But other decisions are difficult and carry life-altering consequences, like starting a family or changing jobs or moving to another state. We would be wise to follow Esther's lead and seek the advice of others in our action plans and then ask for prayer support if we decide to move forward.

Step 3: Take Deliberate Action

Once we know the next right thing to do, we shouldn't hesitate. Take deliberate action. Esther did. After three days, she went in to the king, presented her request, and pointed the finger at Haman.

A word of caution here: we can't wait to act until we are 100 percent certain of the outcome. If Esther had delayed until she was sure about how the king would respond, it might have been too late to save her people. If we can't see clearly ahead, we just take the first step. Then we can move slowly and cautiously, just as we would drive through fog.

I used to live near a large lake with thick early morning fog. Since I had to attend a morning class, I needed to learn how to drive in the fog. I crept along slowly, watching for any traffic. I often thought how much faster and easier my commute would be if there were no fog.

Wouldn't it be great if we had 100 percent visibility in our lives? If we could see our future with perfect clarity, then we could plan more intelligently, move forward with speed and confidence, and avoid collisions with circumstances and people. But if we refuse to act until we have a clear view of our future, we will wait . . . and wait . . . and wait. The important thing is to start moving. Just do the next right thing. And we will find that when we take the first step, even in the fog, things will become clearer.

I encourage you to think of one simple action step and do it. What is the next right thing that God is asking you to do right now? Maybe you are struggling with loneliness—for you, the next right thing would be joining a support group, a Sunday school class, or a Bible study to make some friends. Perhaps you are in a job that provides a good salary but demands you go against your beliefs—for you, the next right thing would be to ask God to lead you to a new position that honors Him. Maybe a friend has turned on you, perhaps for a political belief you have because of your faith. Your next right thing might be to do something kind for that person— bake some cookies, take them to coffee, or invite them over for dinner—to show them the love of Christ.

Whatever you sense God calling you to do, I encourage you to make that phone call, write that letter, accept that invitation, or schedule that appointment. If we step out in faith to do the next right thing, we will be surprised how much easier it will be to take the next step and then the step after that one. As Daniel said, "The people who know their God will display strength and take action" (Dan. 11:32).

Step 4: Leave the Results of Our Action to God

Rarely, if ever, can we control the reactions of other people after we have taken action. Esther could not control how the king would react when she showed up in the throne room unannounced. And once the king granted her life, Esther didn't know how he would respond to her request. There's a good chance we also don't know exactly how something is going to play out once we decide to do the next right thing. It's at these times we must trust God and leave the results in His hands.

This reminds me of the story of a young woman in Scotland who sensed God calling her to teach a Sunday school class for poverty-stricken boys. Each boy was given a new suit to wear to class. The teacher spent hours preparing her weekly lessons and eagerly looked forward to teaching the boys—except for one obstinate child named Bob, who was especially rowdy and disruptive.

After attending the first few classes, Bob did not return. So the teacher went looking for him. When she finally found him, Bob's new suit was dirty and torn. She gave him another new suit, and he came back to Sunday school.

But a few weeks later, Bob quit again. The teacher went back once more to find him. When she did, she was dismayed to discover that Bob had ruined yet another suit. Frustrated, she went to the superintendent. "I'm completely discouraged about Bob," she told him. "I guess we must give up on him."

"Don't do that!" the superintendent pleaded. "I believe there is still hope. Try him one more time."

So they gave Bob a third suit and invited him to come back to class. This time, he began attending regularly. Not long afterward, he became a Christian—and even later taught that same Sunday school class!

That young boy who had seemed to be a lost cause was Robert Morrison, who became the first Protestant missionary to China. He translated the Bible into Chinese and brought the Word of God to millions of people. All because a young Sunday school teacher did not give up on Bob and determined to do the next right thing.[7]

This is why Paul said, "Let us not become weary in doing good, for at the proper time we will reap a harvest if we do not give up" (Gal. 6:9 NIV). As we summon the courage to walk in obedience and press on to do what God is calling us to do, we have to trust God with the results. Soon, we will discover that we have not merely survived in this hostile world but have courageously thrived.

A Final Thought

Never Give Up Hope!

As followers of Jesus, courageously living out our faith in a hostile world sometimes feels like being stranded on a deserted island surrounded by shark-infested waters. We can become physically and spiritually exhausted as we deal with wave after wave of difficult relationships, disappointing circumstances, persistent addictions and sins, and the anxiety and suffering that are an unavoidable part of this life.

Whenever we feel overwhelmed by struggles, the only thing we have left is hope. As believers, we cling to the hope that one day we will be rescued, that relationships will be mended, that sins will be washed away, and that Someone will fix everything that is broken.

As we have seen in this book, you and I can have the courage to thrive regardless of what challenges we encounter when we apply the ten essential survival skills we have learned.

First, *don't panic.* Remember that no matter what you are facing, God is in control. Whenever you are tempted to worry or be afraid, take courage in this unchanging promise: "Greater is He who is in you than he who is in the world" (1 John 4:4).

Second, *gain situational awareness.* Look around and correctly assess the reality of what is happening. Stay awake, keep alert, and be serious-minded as you walk in the way of wisdom and gain awareness of your situation.

Third, *take inventory.* What spiritual gifts, life experiences, and biblical promises has God given you to deal with this circumstance? Take inventory of the tools God has supplied you, and choose ways to apply them to your life.

Fourth, *develop a victor, not a victim mindset.* Resist the temptation to see yourself as a victim of other people's actions or circumstances that are beyond your control. Instead, develop a victor's mindset by following God's ways and trusting His purpose in everything He allows into your life.

Fifth, *trust your training.* Call to mind the Scripture passages you have studied and the biblical promises you know to be true related to your situation. Being able to trust your training by recalling memorized verses during times of temptation can save you from many troubles.

Sixth, *bend, don't break.* During times of conflict, be willing to take steps that lead to peace in a creative and grace-filled manner. If you can do so without compromising your Christian convictions, then you just might "overcome evil with good" (Rom. 12:21).

Seventh, *beware of celebrating the summit.* Be careful not to celebrate your successes too often or too long. Otherwise, you will be tempted to think you did it all on your own. Keep pressing on, and humble yourself to receive the help you need from God and others.

Eighth, *learn from the past.* The issues you face in your life are not unique; others have faced similar challenges. Learn from those who have gone before you, and derive courage from them as you chart a path forward.

Ninth, *help others.* Don't let your desire for self-preservation keep you from seeing the needs of others around you. Instead, seek opportunities to serve others by placing their needs and interests ahead of your own.

Finally, when you've done everything you know how to do and aren't sure how to move forward, simply *do the next right thing.* Take the risk to step out in obedience to God and then press on to do what God is calling you to do, trusting Him with the results.

These ten survival skills are essential to navigating the difficult and often treacherous terrain of today's world. But all the tools and training—all the survival tips we've covered in this book—will be of no use to us if we lose hope.

Hope is the one virtue of the Christian faith that, if lost, "makes the heart sick" (Prov. 13:12). Without hope, mountaineers never complete their climbs. Without hope, prisoners of war give in and become traitors. Without hope, castaways lose their minds and wish for death to come. Without hope, explorers lose their way. Without hope, addicts lose their will, artists lose their creativity, teachers lose their voice, couples lose their love, families lose their joy, and churches lose their purpose.

Perhaps no one understands the importance of hope better than Florence Chadwick. On July 4, 1952, this thirty-four-year-old competitive swimmer waded into the waters of the Pacific Ocean. Her goal was to become the first woman to swim the twenty-one miles from Catalina Island to the California coast.

Chadwick was an experienced long-distance swimmer. She had already become the first woman to swim the English Channel in both directions. Her biggest challenge in the Pacific Ocean that day was not the distance but the bone-chilling waters and the thick fog that made it almost impossible for her to see anything, including the boats accompanying her.

While Americans watched on television, Chadwick swam for hours in the numbing water and choppy waves. But the fog kept Chadwick from seeing her goal, and she lost hope of ever reaching the shore. When she begged to be taken out, her mother and her trainer, who were in one of the support boats, cheered her on. But after fifteen hours and fifty-five minutes, Chadwick stopped swimming and was pulled out— only to discover that she had quit less than a mile from the coast. She told a reporter, "If I could have seen land I know I could have made it."[1]

Two months later, she attempted the feat again. Once again, a thick fog obscured the coastline, and she couldn't see the shore. But this time, she made it because she kept reminding herself that the land was there. With that confidence, she bravely swam on and achieved her goal. In fact, she broke the men's record by more than two hours!

Can you relate to Florence Chadwick's first attempt? All too often, we find ourselves in a fog of worry, doubt, depression, health problems, loneliness, financial uncertainty, and strained relationships. There is no end in sight, and we are tempted to give up hope. But we must not quit! Land is just ahead.

Until we reach the shoreline, the Bible tells us that we should not despair. Just because our lives appear to be spinning out of control at times doesn't mean they really are out of control. We may not be able to see the future clearly, but our sovereign God does. The psalmist declares, "The LORD has established His throne in the heavens, and His sovereignty rules over all" (Ps. 103:19).

Our God knows our future because He has planned our future. Until the fog of uncertainty lifts and the waves of adversity eventually subside, we can follow the command of Psalm 27:14: "Wait for the LORD; be strong and let your heart take courage; yes, wait for the LORD."

You and I can go forward in life with courage, even though we may be "afflicted in every way, but not crushed; perplexed, but not despairing; persecuted, but not forsaken; struck down, but not destroyed" (2 Cor. 4:8–9). Like the apostle Paul, who was "always of good courage" no matter what he faced in life, we too can courageously face whatever evil comes our way, knowing that the One "who delivered us from so great a peril of death . . . will deliver us, He on whom we have set our hope" (5:6; 1:10).

If we believe that and never give up hope, then no matter what comes in our lives, we will do more than survive—we will thrive!

Notes

Survival Tip #1 Don't Panic

1. Quotations taken from Ben Sherwood, *The Survivors Club: The Secrets and Science That Could Save Your Life* (New York: Grand Central, 2009), 66–68. See also David H. Koch, "Passenger's Account of Escape from Burning Boeing 737 Highlights Cabin Safety Issues," *Flight Safety Foundation Cabin Crew Safety* 8, no. 3 (May/June 1993): https://flightsafety.org/ccs/ccs_may-jun93.pdf; and The Week Staff, "The Last Word: They Lived to Tell the Tale," *The Week*, February 13, 2009, https://theweek.com/articles/508512/last-word-lived-tell-tale.

2. Among survivalists, this is known as the 10-80-10 Theory. For more information, see Sherwood, *Survivors Club*, 44–49.

3. See Dr. Henry Irving, "Keep Calm and Carry On—The Compromise behind the Slogan," *History of Government*, June 27, 2014, https://history.blog.gov.uk/2014/06/27/keep-calm-and-carry-on-the-compromise-behind-the-slogan/.

4. Robert Robinson, "Come, Thou Fount of Every Blessing," 1757, public domain.

5. C. S. Lewis, *Mere Christianity* (San Francisco: HarperSanFrancisco, 2001), 46.

6. Robert Jeffress, *Grace Gone Wild: Getting a Grip on God's Amazing Gift* (Colorado Springs: WaterBrook Press, 2005), 10.

7. Warren W. Wiersbe, "Judges," *The Wiersbe Bible Commentary: The Complete Old Testament in One Volume* (Colorado Springs: David C. Cook, 2007), 445.

8. Seth Godin, "Risk, Fear, and Worry," *Seth's Blog*, January 24, 2012, https://seths.blog/2012/07/risk-fear-and-worry.

9. Peter Kreeft, *Back to Virtue: Traditional Moral Wisdom for Modern Moral Confusion* (San Francisco: Ignatius Press, 1992), 105.

10. Mark Batterson, *All In: You Are One Decision Away from a Totally Different Life* (Grand Rapids: Zondervan, 2013), 13.

Survival Tip #2 Gain Situational Awareness

1. Kyle Dickman, "19: The True Story of the Yarnell Hill Fire," *Outside Magazine*, September 17, 2013, https://www.outsideonline.com/1926426/19-true-story -yarnell-hill-fire. All subsequent quotations about the Yarnell Hill Fire come from this source.

2. "Trump's Faith-Based Address Encourages Nation after Las Vegas: Pastor Jeffress," *Fox Business*, October 3, 2017, https://video.foxbusiness.com/v/55972 03697001/#sp=show-clips.

3. Georgiann Davis, "More People Are Identifying As Trans and Gender Nonconforming. Why?" *Houston Chronicle*, July 9, 2018, https://www.houstonchron icle.com/local/gray-matters/article/u-s-increase-trans-gender-nonconforming -people-13054716.php.

4. Garin Flowers, "'Transracial' Man, Born White, Says He Feels Filipino," *USA Today*, November 15, 2017, https://www.usatoday.com/story/news/nation -now/2017/11/13/transracial-man-born-white-says-he-feels-filipino/858043001/.

5. Lucia I. Suarez Sang, "Dutch Businessman, 69, Seeks to Legally Identify As 20 Years Younger," *Fox News*, https://www.foxnews.com/world/dutch-business man-69-seeks-to-legally-identify-as-20-years-younger.

6. Gavia Baker-Whitelaw, "Understanding the Otherkin," *The Kernel*, February 22, 2015, https://kernelmag.dailydot.com/issue-sections/features-issue-sec tions/11866/otherkin-tumblr-definition-pronouns/.

7. Robert Jeffress, *Countdown to the Apocalypse* (Nashville: FaithWords, 2015), 96.

8. "Barth in Retirement," *Time*, May 31, 1963, http://content.time.com/time /subscriber/article/0,33009,896838,00.html.

9. Fred Smith, *You and Your Network* (Waco: Key-Word, 1984), 89.

10. Mike Pence, "Remarks by Vice President Pence at Liberty University's Commencement," Lynchburg, Virginia, May 11, 2019, https://www.whitehouse .gov/briefings-statements/remarks-vice-president-pence-liberty-universitys -commencement/.

Survival Tip #3 Take Inventory

1. James A. Lovell, "Houston, We've Had a Problem," NASA History, accessed July 18, 2019, https://history.nasa.gov/SP-350/ch-13-1.html.

2. D. Martin Lloyd-Jones, *The Christian Warfare* (Grand Rapids: Baker Books, 1977), 42.

3. Robert Jeffress, *The Divine Defense: Six Simple Strategies for Winning Your Greatest Battles* (Colorado Springs: WaterBrook, 2006), 111.

4. Eugene Peterson, *A Long Obedience in the Same Direction: Discipleship in an Instant Society*, 20th anniversary ed. (Downers Grove, IL: IVP, 2000).

5. Content in this section adapted from Robert Jeffress, *Divine Defense*, 144–45.

6. Romans 16:1–16, Colossians 4:7–17, and 2 Timothy 4:19–21 include the names of others who ministered to Paul.

Survival Tip #4 Develop a Victor, Not a Victim Mindset

1. Ernest Shackleton, as quoted in Caroline Alexander, "Epic of Survival: Shackleton," *National Geographic* 194, no. 5 (November 1998): 92.

2. Shackleton, as quoted in Alexander, "Epic of Survival," 92.

3. As quoted in Carl Hopkins Elmore, *Quit You Like Men* (New York: Charles Scribner's Sons, 1944), 53. Shackleton's advertisement is likely apocryphal, since archives of the *London Times* show no such advertisement.

4. Raymond Priestley, as quoted in Alfred Lansing, *Endurance: Shackleton's Incredible Voyage* (New York: Carrol and Graf, 2003), 13–14.

5. Ernest Shackleton, *The Heart of the Antarctic: Being the Story of the British Antarctic Expedition, 1907–1909* (London: William Heinemann, 1909), 321.

6. Charles R. Swindoll, "The Value of a Positive Attitude," *Insight for Today: A Daily Devotional by Chuck Swindoll*, November 19, 2015, https://www.insight.org/resources/daily-devotional/individual/the-value-of-a-positive-attitude.

7. Dennis Davidson, "How to Dwell in Jesus's Love," *Sermon Central*, November 2, 2009, https://www.sermoncentral.com/sermons/how-to-dwell-in-jesus-love-dennis-davidson-sermon-on-god-s-love-140742?page=1&wc=800.

8. "Bulldog Spirit—A National Myth?" *K9 Magazine* 70 (December 17, 2013), http://www.k9magazine.com/bulldog-spirit-national-myth/.

Survival Tip #5 Trust Your Training

1. Chesley Sullenberger, as quoted in Scott McCartney, "Crash Courses for the Crew," *Wall Street Journal*, January 27, 2009, https://www.wsj.com/articles/SB123301773654017857.

2. Chesley Sullenberger, as quoted in Rachel Cooke, "Chesley Sullenberger: An Old-Fashioned Kind of Hero," *The Guardian*, November 27, 2016, http://www.theguardian.com/film/2016/nov/27/chesley-sullenberger-sully-film-clint-eastwood-tom-hanks-miracle-hudson-river.

3. Harry Suhartono, Alan Levin, and Julie Johnsson, "Boeing Jet's Faulty Sensor Wasn't Fixed before Lion Air Crash, Report Finds," *Bloomberg*, November 27, 2018, https://www.bloomberg.com/news/articles/2018-11-27/lion-air-pilots-struggle-detailed-in-preliminary-crash-report.

4. I'm grateful for my colleague and collaborator Derrick Jeter for many of the ideas and much of the structure of the material in this chapter. Adapted from Derrick G. Jeter, "The Why and How of Scripture Memory," sermon, Coffee House Fellowship, Stonebriar Community Church, Frisco, Texas, May 24, 2015.

5. Dr. Dan Morris, "How Memory Works," *Ministry 127*, January 22, 2011, http://ministry127.com/christian-living/how-memory-works.

6. Simon J. Kistemaker, *New Testament Commentary: Exposition of the Epistles of Peter and Epistle of Jude* (Grand Rapids: Baker, 1987), comments on Jude 1:17; as quoted in "Memorizing His Word," https://www.preceptaustin.org/memorizing_his_word.

7. Darlene Deibler Rose, *Evidence Not Seen: A Woman's Miraculous Faith in the Jungles of World War II*, repr. ed. (New York: HarperCollins, 1990), 143.

8. Martin Luther, *Faith Alone: A Daily Devotional*, ed. James C. Galvin (Grand Rapids: Zondervan, 2005), March 8.

9. Jeff Bridges, as quoted in Andy Greene, "The Last Word: Jeff Bridges on Dylan, the Dude and Surviving Box-Office Duds," *Rolling Stone*, September 2016, https://www.rollingstone.com/movies/movie-features/the-last-word-jeff-bridges-on-dylan-the-dude-and-surviving-box-office-duds-250631/.

Survival Tip #6 Bend, Don't Break

1. All quotations come from Jonathan Franklin, *438 Days*, as excerpted in *Reader's Digest*, accessed June 10, 2019, https://www.rd.com/true-stories/survival/man-stranded-sea-438-days/.

2. Martin Luther King Jr., "Where Do We Go from Here: Annual Report to the 11th Convention of the Southern Christian Leadership Conference, August 16, 1967, Atlanta, Georgia," *A Testament of Hope: The Essential Writings and Speeches of Martin Luther King, Jr.*, ed. James M. Washington (New York: HarperCollins, 1991), 250.

3. Stephen Olford, *The Grace of Giving*, rev. ed. (Grand Rapids: Kregel, 2000), 52; https://bible.org/illustration/grace-giving.

4. See Robert Jeffress, *Twilight's Last Gleaming: How America's Last Days Can Be Your Best Days* (Brentwood: Worthy Publishing, 2011), 206–7.

5. Thomas Merton, as quoted in Peter Kreeft, *Back to Virtue: Traditional Moral Wisdom for Modern Moral Confusion* (San Francisco: Ignatius Press, 1992), 146.

6. Martin Luther King Jr., "Letter from Birmingham City Jail (1963)," accessed June 17, 2019, University of Warwick, https://warwick.ac.uk/fac/arts/english/currentstudents/undergraduate/modules/fulllist/special/en304/2016-17/martin_luther_king_letter_from_birmingham_jail.pdf.

Survival Tip #7 Beware of Celebrating the Summit

1. Doug Hansen, as quoted in Jon Krakauer, *Into Thin Air: A Personal Account of the Mt. Everest Disaster* (New York: Villard, 1997), 68.

2. It is presumed that Hansen fell to his death because, on May 23, two climbers on another expedition found Hansen's ice ax but did not find his body.

3. Krakauer, *Into Thin Air*, 181.

4. C. S. Lewis, *Mere Christianity* (San Francisco: HarperSanFrancisco, 2001), 124.

5. Peter Kreeft, *Back to Virtue: Traditional Moral Teaching for Modern Moral Confusion* (San Francisco: Ignatius Press, 1992), 100, emphasis in original.

6. Dallas Willard, *The Divine Conspiracy* (New York: Harper, 1998), 100.

7. Andrew Murray, *Humility: The Journey toward Holiness* (Minneapolis: Bethany House, 2001), 55.

8. Joel Belz, "Muscle and Restraint," *World*, August 30, 2018, https://world .wng.org/2018/08/muscle_and_restraint.

9. David Mamet, *The Untouchables*, screenplay (Hollywood, CA: Paramount Pictures, 1987).

10. David Breashears, as quoted in Krakauer, *Into Thin Air*, 277.

Survival Tip #8 Learn from the Past

1. All quotations come from Sally Williams, "Sole Survivor: The Woman Who Fell to Earth," *The Telegraph*, March 22, 2012, https://www.telegraph.co.uk/cul ture/books/authorinterviews/9143701/Sole-survivor-the-woman-who-fell-to -earth.html.

2. Juliane Koepcke, as quoted in Katherine MacDonald, "Survival Stories: The Girl Who Fell from the Sky," *Reader's Digest*, accessed June 10, 2019, https:// www.rd.com/true-stories/survival/survival-stories-the-girl-who-fell-from-the-sky/.

3. Patrick Riccards, "National Survey Finds Just 1 in 3 Americans Would Pass Citizenship Test," The Woodrow Wilson National Fellowship Foundation, October 3, 2018, https://woodrow.org/news/national-survey-finds-just-1-in-3 -americans-would-pass-citizenship-test/.

4. Riccards, "National Survey Finds Just 1 in 3 Americans Would Pass Citizenship Test."

5. Aislinn Simpson, "Winston Churchill Didn't Really Exist, Say Teens," *The Telegraph*, February 4, 2008, https://www.telegraph.co.uk/news/uknews/1577511 /Winston-Churchill-didnt-really-exist-say-teens.html.

6. George Santayana, *Life of Reason, or the Phases of Human Progress*, vol. 1 (New York: Charles Scribner's Sons, 1905), 284.

7. Martin Luther, as quoted in "Martin Luther—The Early Years," *Christian History* 34, https://www.christianitytoday.com/history/issues/issue-34/colorful -sayings-of-colorful-luther.html.

8. Doris Kearns Goodwin, *Leadership: In Turbulent Times* (New York: Simon & Schuster, 2018).

9. Thomas Carlyle, as quoted in Peter H. Gibbon, *A Call to Heroism: Renewing America's Vision of Greatness* (New York: Atlantic Monthly Press, 2002), 19.

10. Adapted from David Peach, "10 Famous Christian Missionaries," *What Christians Want to Know*, accessed June 10, 2019, https://www.whatchristians wanttoknow.com/10-famous-christian-missionaries/.

11. Bernard R. DeRemer, "Victorian Missionary: Amy Carmichael," *Disciple*, October 2005, http://www.disciplemagazine.com/www/articles/222.1526.

Survival Tip #9 Help Others

1. *Schindler's List*, Blu-ray, directed by Steven Spielberg (1993; Universal City, CA: Universal Pictures, 2013).

2. Marla Diamond, "WCBS 880 9/11 Series: Brian Clark Escaped the Twin Towers from Above the Impact Line," *CBS New York*, September 6, 2011, https://newyork.cbslocal.com/2011/09/06/wcbs-880-911-series-brian-clark-escaped-the-twin-towers-from-above-the-impact-line/.

3. WBUR, "9/11 Survivor Brian Clark Reflects on His Escape, 15 Years Later," *Here and Now*, September 7, 2016, https://www.wbur.org/hereandnow/2016/09/07/911-survivor-brian-clark.

4. Billy Graham, "The Smallness of the Self," *Leadership 5*, no. 2, as quoted in *Preaching Today*, June 1996, https://www.preachingtoday.com/illustrations/1996/june/149.html.

5. Rummana Hussain, "Passengers Give Up Seats So Soldiers Can Go First-Class," newsbull.com, July 16, 2004, as quoted in Craig Brian Larson and Phyllis Ten Elshof, *1001 Illustrations That Connect* (Grand Rapids: Zondervan, 2009), 489–90.

6. Winston S. Churchill, as quoted in *Churchill by Himself: The Definitive Collection of Quotations*, ed. Richard Langworth (New York: Public Affairs, 2008), 13.

7. Rebecca Everett, "How a Heartbroken Doomsday Prepper Who Lost Everything Is Now Saving Hurricane Victims," NJ.com, October 1, 2017, https://www.nj.com/burlington/index.ssf/2017/09/how_a_heartbroken_doomsday_prepper_who_lost_everyt.html.

8. C. S. Lewis, *The Weight of Glory* (New York: HarperCollins, 2009), 46, emphasis in original.

9. Philip Yancey, *The Jesus I Never Knew* (Grand Rapids: Zondervan, 2002), 39.

10. Carl Menninger, as quoted in Thomas L. Constable, "Notes on Philippians," accessed June 25, 2019, https://www.planobiblechapel.org/tcon/notes/html/nt/philippians/philippians.htm.

Survival Tip #10 Do the Next Right Thing

1. All quotations come from James B. Stockdale, "The World of Epictetus," *Atlantic Monthly*, April 1978 (repr., McLean, VA: The Trinity Forum, 2010), 8, 14, 18.

2. Jim Collins, *Good to Great: Why Some Companies Make the Leap and Others Don't* (New York: HarperBusiness, 2001), 84.

3. Collins, *Good to Great*, 85.

4. Epictetus, "Encheiridion," *The Discourses Books III–IV, Fragments, Encheiridion 1*, trans. W. A. Oldfather (Cambridge, MA: Harvard University Press, 1928), 483.

5. David Jeremiah, *Signs of Life: Back to the Basics of Authentic Christianity* (Nashville: Thomas Nelson, 2007), 150.

6. Billy Graham and National Association of Evangelicals, "An Evangelical Manifesto: A Strategic Plan for the Dawn of the 21st Century," as quoted in Kenneth B. Mulholland and Gary Corwin, eds., *Working Together with God*

to *Shape the New Millennium: Opportunities and Limitations* (Pasadena, CA: William Carey Library, 2000), 111.

7. H. G. Bosch, *Our Daily Bread* (Grand Rapids: RBC Ministries), as quoted in "Third Time's the Charm!" *Precept Austin*, July 28, 2017, https://www.pre ceptaustin.org/galatians_devotionals_2.

A Final Thought

1. Channel Swimming Association, "Queen of the Channel: Florence Chad-wick," accessed June 10, 2019, http://www.queenofthechannel.com/florence -chadwick.

About the Author

Dr. Robert Jeffress is senior pastor of the fourteen-thousand-member First Baptist Church, Dallas, Texas, and a Fox News contributor. He is also an adjunct professor at Dallas Theological Seminary. Dr. Jeffress has made more than two thousand guest appearances on various radio and television programs and regularly appears on major mainstream media outlets such as Fox News channel's *Fox and Friends*, *The O'Reilly Factor*, *Hannity*, *Lou Dobbs Tonight*, *Varney and Co.*, and *Judge Jeanine*; ABC's *Good Morning America*; and HBO's *Real Time with Bill Maher*. Dr. Jeffress hosts a daily radio program, *Pathway to Victory*, that is heard nationwide on over eight hundred stations in major markets such as Dallas–Fort Worth, New York City, Chicago, Los Angeles, Washington, DC, Houston, and Seattle. His weekly television program can be seen in 195 countries and on 11,283 cable and satellite systems throughout the world, including China, and on the Trinity Broadcasting Network and Daystar.

Dr. Jeffress is the author of over twenty books, including *Choosing the Extraordinary Life*, *When Forgiveness Doesn't Make Sense*, *Countdown to the Apocalypse*, and *Not All Roads Lead to Heaven*. Dr. Jeffress recently led his congregation in the completion of a $135 million re-creation of its downtown campus. The project is the largest in modern church history and serves as a "spiritual oasis" covering six blocks of downtown Dallas.

Dr. Jeffress has a DMin from Southwestern Baptist Theological Seminary, a ThM from Dallas Theological Seminary, and a BS from Baylor University. In May 2010 he was awarded a Doctor of Divinity degree from Dallas Baptist University, and in June 2011 he received the Distinguished Alumnus of the Year award from Southwestern Baptist Theological Seminary.

Dr. Jeffress and his wife, Amy, have two daughters, Julia and Dorothy, and a son-in-law, Ryan Sadler.

NOT ALL ROADS LEAD TO HEAVEN

Resources available include...

» The paperback book *Not All Roads Lead to Heaven* plus "Christianity, Cults & Religions"—a side-by-side comparison chart of sixteen groups

» The complete, unedited series on DVD/CD

» A comprehensive ten-week Bible study guidebook, complete with answers to study questions and expanded responses to key points

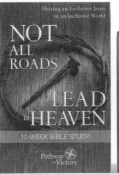
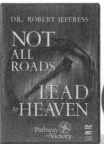

445 0991
YEI

A PLACE CALLED
HEAVEN
FOR KIDS

Colorfully illustrated and using simple concepts and language
that children can understand, *A Place Called Heaven for Kids* gives
children peace of mind about their lost loved one as well as a
comforting, biblical picture of their forever home.

**AVAILABLE WHEREVER BOOKS
AND EBOOKS ARE SOLD**

Choosing the
Extraordinary
Life

God's Secrets for Success and Significance

Resources available include...

» *Choosing the Extraordinary Life* in hardcover or paperback plus "The Elijah Map"—a companion brochure that shows key events in the life of Elijah.

» The complete, unedited series on DVD/CD

YE1   928 445—